THINKING
SIMPLY ABOUT
ADDICTION

THINKING SIMPLY ABOUT ADDICTION

A HANDBOOK FOR RECOVERY

Richard S. Sandor, M.D.

JEREMY P. TARCHER/PENGUIN

a member of Penguin Group (USA) Inc.

New York

JEREMY P. TARCHER/PENGUIN
Published by the Penguin Group
Penguin Group (USA) Inc., 375 Hudson Street, New York, New York 10014, USA •
Penguin Group (Canada), 90 Eglinton Avenue East, Suite 700, Toronto, Ontario M4P 2Y3,
Canada (a division of Pearson Canada Inc.) • Penguin Books Ltd, 80 Strand, London WC2R 0RL,
England • Penguin Ireland, 25 St Stephen's Green, Dublin 2, Ireland (a division of Penguin Books
Ltd) • Penguin Group (Australia), 250 Camberwell Road, Camberwell, Victoria 3124, Australia
(a division of Pearson Australia Group Pty Ltd) • Penguin Books India Pvt Ltd, 11 Community
Centre, Panchsheel Park, New Delhi–110 017, India • Penguin Group (NZ), 67 Apollo Drive,
Rosedale, North Shore 0632, New Zealand (a division of Pearson New Zealand Ltd) •
Penguin Books (South Africa) (Pty) Ltd, 24 Sturdee Avenue, Rosebank, Johannesburg 2196,
South Africa

Penguin Books Ltd, Registered Offices: 80 Strand, London WC2R 0RL, England

Most Tarcher/Penguin books are available at special quantity discounts for bulk purchase for sales
promotions, premiums, fund-raising, and educational needs. Special books or book excerpts also can
be created to fit specific needs. For details, write Penguin Group (USA) Inc. Special Markets,
375 Hudson Street, New York, NY 10014.

Library of Congress Cataloging-in-Publication Data

Sandor, Richard S.
Thinking simply about addiction : a handbook for recovery / Richard S. Sandor.
p.   cm.
Includes bibliographical references and index.
ISBN 978-1-58542-688-1
1. Drug addiction—Treatment.   2. Alcoholism—Treatment.   I. Title.
HV5801.S31397   2009   2008054716
362.29'18—dc22

Printed in the United States of America
1 3 5 7 9 10 8 6 4 2

BOOK DESIGN BY NICOLE LAROCHE

Contents

Preface

A few years ago I had a spectacular lesson in the value of thinking simply. I had hiked several miles into the local mountains for a day of wilderness trout fishing. At the beginning of the day, the sky was clear, but it was also unusually humid, and by noon ominous thunderclouds had begun to gather overhead. The sky grew dark, and the air took on a prickly stillness. Then came the startling hiss of a lightning strike on the ridge just above me, followed almost instantly by the roar of thunder. It occurred to me that perhaps I ought to turn around and head home.

I knew it was going to rain, but I wasn't concerned about getting wet. The day was still warm, and I had already spent several hours crisscrossing the stream, wading up to my waist. And I wasn't worried about being hit by lightning; I was too deep in the canyon for that. But images of a flash flood began to flit through my mind—tons of water, mud, and debris tearing down the canyon and carrying me and everything else away in its path—and that was scary.

I remembered having read that wet graphite was an excellent electrical conductor, so prudently I took down my fly rod, wrapped it in its cloth cover, stuffed the aluminum reel into my vest, and started hiking back downstream. Then, the rain began, and it wasn't the usual Southern California pitter-patter. Instead, it was just what I feared: a drenching, sheets-of-solid-water downpour that our sparsely forested slopes cannot absorb. Another bolt of lightning struck the ridge, and a clatter of boulders tumbled down a few yards ahead of me. I began to feel a panic rise in my chest.

And then the lesson came to me.

If I would simply pay attention to each step, I would not slip on a wet rock. If I did not slip on a wet rock, I would not fall. If I did not fall, I would not hit my head and drown unconscious in the stream. Nor would I break a leg and die overnight of exposure. All I had to do was to watch where I put my foot each time I took a step. Simple. And if I quietly minded my own business in this way, doing what was really up to me and me alone to do, I might even hear the roar of a flash flood if one was headed my way and perhaps have a chance to climb to safety. Time slowed down and became my ally. There was no need to rush, no need to get hurt. I simply had to pay attention to each step. Sure enough, about two hours and six thousand steps later, the rain stopped, the sun reappeared, and I emerged from the canyon. And there was my car, just where I had left it, ready to take me home.

That's what I mean by thinking simply, and my intention in this book is to apply the same principle to thinking about addiction. Of course, there is the very real danger of inadvertently slipping into simplistic thinking, the kind of anti-intellectual attitude that discounts complexity in order to avoid what can sometimes be genuinely difficult. I'll do my best to avoid it and the smug confidence it breeds. By contrast, thinking simply, in the sense I'm aiming for, demands humility. It means accepting complexity as the only path to what you are trying to understand: all the trees you have to wander among, perhaps even lost, until you begin to get a sense of the forest as a whole. For thinking simply about addiction, that means listening carefully to alcoholics and drug addicts talk about what they actually experience. In time, despite all the differences in their stories, a common theme begins to emerge. The essential nature of addiction appears, and the path to recovery becomes clear.

Of course, my lesson that day in the mountains didn't come from nothing. It was the result of having spent hundreds of days in the world of terrain and trails, and thousands of hours bearing witness to the wilderness of my own unruly thoughts and feelings. The same is true of this book and what I want to say about addiction: It's the result of more than twenty-five years of working with addicts and alcoholics as a physician, medical director, teacher, and administrator. For the sake of honesty, however, I should confess that fate had to drag me, more or less kicking and screaming, into it.

In 1980, when I was first given the opportunity to become the medical director of an alcohol treatment program, I refused. My experience with such patients in the ER and psych ward wasn't the sort of thing I could imagine looking forward to as a steady diet. But circumstances conspired to change my mind, and only a few days later I found it necessary to accept the position and did—warily.

As part of my duties, I was to give a weekly lecture to the patients. The program director gave me an outline to follow, but it was the standard "The bad things that will happen to your health if you keep on drinking" pap that turns the doctor into a poorly disguised preacher. It bored me, and I had little confidence that it would do the patients much good. Instead, I held question-and-answer sessions and slowly began to hear what the patients needed to tell me and what I needed to say to try to help them understand.

In addition to my lecture duties, I also began to supervise the treatment staff and, again slowly, began to realize that, although there was plenty of goodwill, our whole approach seemed limited and strangely rigid. When a patient didn't want to cooperate with our mode of treatment, almost everyone wanted to discharge him. The real motive was concealed in some form of psychobabble, but the truth was we didn't know what to do with people who were defiant, hostile, or otherwise resistant to our suggestions, and we didn't like being made to feel incompetent. Then, just to make things even more confusing, there were the compliant patients who followed our treatment plans faithfully but then relapsed shortly after discharge anyway.

Into this confusion there appeared help in the unlikely form of a new clinical director, a bearded, burly, and gruff Bostonian who was an ex-con (he'd listed his educational qualifications for the job as "Jackson State," the Michigan penitentiary) and recovering alcoholic. This man, Tom Redgate, sized me up, ventured that I "might be educable," and hauled me off to AA meetings. And slowly a transformation began to work itself into my understanding. At these meetings I heard the stories of hundreds of people who'd gotten sober without any professional help whatever, and the dim light of comprehension began to dawn in my mind. Listening to people talk about their experiences in *recovering* from addiction, about which I'd learned nothing in all my excellent academic education, I began to understand what addiction was.

It's now four medical directorships, several dozen professional conferences, scores of presentations, hundreds of staff meetings, and thousands of patients later, and I've adapted my original talks with patients to meet the needs of the different audiences (both professional and lay) I've spoken with over the years. But, essentially, the thoughts expressed in this book remain rooted in the histories of the many alcoholics and addicts with whom I have worked. Happily, virtually everything I have come to understand clinically has been verified scientifically, at least as I interpret it, in *The Natural History of Alcoholism* by George Vaillant. This beautifully written and compelling study has been mandatory reading in all the courses I have taught on the subject, and I will refer to it often.

My own little book is arranged in four chapters around four questions I have been asked time and time again, and not only by my patients but also by their families, my colleagues, and the lay public. Condensed, they are as follows:

1. Is addiction a disease?
2. Why me?

3. Does treatment "work"?
4. Is a spiritual awakening necessary for recovery?

By way of preview, these are my equally condensed responses:

1. Yes, addictions are diseases. Specifically, they are disorders of automaticity.

2. Why *not* you? To be human is to be susceptible to addiction, though some people are more susceptible to some addictions than to others.

3. Work on its own? No. The idea that treatment can "work," while the alcoholic or addict himself doesn't, completely misses what recovery from addiction means.

4. And finally, yes, a spiritual awakening of some kind is necessary for recovery. For abstinence, no, but for recovery, yes.

Obviously, I've got some explaining to do, and although I intend these explanations first for alcoholics and addicts themselves, I believe they will be useful for their families and for clinicians as well. But beyond these audiences, thinking simply about addiction is important for all of us, because, in the end, recovery from addiction teaches the same timeless lessons that bring meaning to all human suffering, lessons we would all do well to learn.

Finally, let me say that this is not an academic work, and I haven't cited all my references individually as would be required in a scholarly book. Where scientific evidence confirms what I have learned from my patients, I use it; where it does not, I try to understand why. In any case, I make no great claims of originality. Many of the ideas in this book have come from someone else, and in order to acknowledge their efforts, I include a general bibliography for each chapter. I hope that will repay my debt.

THINKING
SIMPLY ABOUT
ADDICTION

Chapter One

IS ADDICTION
A DISEASE?

INTRODUCTION

Alcoholics and drug addicts are hard to understand. They even
baffle themselves as much as they mystify the rest of us. They get
into terrible trouble, beg for help, and then squander our care by
getting drunk or loaded again. In time, their friends and families
give up in despair. Doctors, nurses, and therapists become bitter
and "burn out." The addict himself ends up, as it is put in AA,
in a state of "incomprehensible demoralization." What's wrong
with these people? Why do they repeatedly go back to something that is so obviously bad for them? Why can't they control
themselves? Are they morally weak? Fundamentally selfish and
self-defeating? Or just plain stupid?

The modern view is that addiction is a disease, a disorder

rooted in brain chemistry. But not everyone agrees, and even those who are convinced have trouble defending their beliefs against intelligent dissent. After all, the critics argue, if alcoholics and addicts were the helpless victims of a disease, no one would ever recover. How can you claim to be both "powerless over alcohol" (the first step of AA) and yet, at the same time, assert that recovery is based on choosing not to drink "one day at a time"? You can't have it both ways. Either you are responsible for your drinking or you're not.

At first sight, this either/or argument seems reasonable, but it's based on an error. Behavior has been confused with a disease: *doing something* (drinking, using) with *having something* (the addiction). And while the two are related, they are not the same thing. Obviously, no one can become addicted (i.e., get the disease) without drinking or using a drug (behavior), but addictions develop over time, and what starts out as a *cause* of the disease later becomes its *manifestation*.

This difference between cause and appearance is the same in other diseases. You can't develop pneumonia, for example, without being exposed to a germ, but as the germs multiply, the disease becomes manifest in symptoms: fever, cough, chest pain, shortness of breath. The disease isn't simply more and more germs; it's also the body's reaction to those germs, what we call the "inflammatory response." In the same way, what begins as the choice to drink or use a drug may later become something else, something no one chooses—a psychophysiological reaction that has a life of its own—an addiction. At that point, the addict's drinking or using behavior has become the manifestation of the disease, not the disease itself. He may look like he's making choices, but where it really counts, something else is in charge.

Meanwhile, despite the confusion and controversy swirling around the disease concept of addiction, the neuroscientists consider the matter settled or irrelevant and forge ahead with their own agenda, delving deeper and deeper into the biochemistry of the alcoholic and drug-addicted brain, endlessly promising a "cure" and yet never quite delivering the goods. What is missing, and sorely needed, is a clear and comprehensible explanation of what addiction is and why it is a disease. That's what this book is about.

The essential idea I'm presenting is that addictions are diseases of automaticity—automatisms—developments in the central nervous system that cannot be eliminated but can be rendered dormant. Starting from that idea, all the general features of addiction can be understood in a relatively uncomplicated way, without recourse to expert knowledge gained in the lab or the clinic: why some substances are addictive and others are not, why some people become addicted and others do not, how substance use and misuse differ from addiction, and, most important, why abstinence is necessary for recovery.

Virtually all readers will be familiar with the word *automatic,* from which the words *automaticity* and *automatism* are derived. Think of your car. In the early days of automobiles, the driver had to change gears by hand, as it is said, "manually." It took some skill to work the clutch pedal and gear shift lever correctly, and some people never got it. But then, in 1940, Oldsmobile bypassed the whole problem by introducing the *automatic* transmission—the gears shifted themselves—and all the driver had to decide was whether to go forward or back.

The word *automatic* itself comes from two roots in ancient Greek: *auto*, for "self," and *matos*, "thinking" or "animated." So things that are automatic (or display automaticity) have a life of their own: Once set in motion, they go on by themselves, without any particular intention or attention on our part.

There isn't anything abnormal about automaticity as such; all sorts of things go on in us by themselves (walking, talking, speaking, etc.) once we have taken the decision to start them. In fact, our lives would be impossible without these and many more automatisms. But in addiction, this normal human quality becomes attached to the use of particular toxic substances: alcohol, heroin, cocaine, nicotine, etc. And if an addiction is allowed to grow unchecked, it brings more and more harm to the person who has it and is therefore correctly understood as a disease. Many otherwise normal physiological processes become diseases in just the same way. No one can live, for example, without having a normal blood pressure. But if that pressure gets too high, it begins to destroy the organs it was meant to support and becomes the disease we call hypertension.

The confusion between *doing something* (again, behavior) and *having something* (a disease) is also why it is so hard for people who don't have an addiction to understand those who do. We see people doing something we ourselves do (or, at least, might do but choose not to) and then tend to think that their inner experience must be the same as ours. Take me, for example. I drink. I don't lose control over it. I don't crash my car,

4

lose my job, wreck my health, and terrify my wife and children over it. Then I see my alcoholic friend (wife, son, daughter, nephew, niece . . .) drinking and assume he's just like me. Starting with that assumption, I naturally figure that his inability to control himself must be the result of a weak will or a lack of sound judgment. It's obvious. What's all this nonsense about it being a disease?

But behavior may or may not reflect a person's inner experience. We only know what's going on inside another person by what they tell us about it, and they themselves may not know why they can't drink like other people or why they can't use drugs casually. It's rarely for lack of having tried. Something different goes on inside an alcoholic or drug addict when they drink or use, something you could never discover by watching their behavior and comparing it to your own. You would have to listen to them to understand.

Over a period of about thirty years now, I have listened to several thousand alcoholics and addicts describe what it's like to be addicted, and as the old medical proverb says: "If you listen hard enough, the patient will tell you what's wrong with him." What my patients have told me is that the core experience of being addicted is *powerlessness*, the experience of having *lost control* over the use of alcohol or a drug. In each case, the beginning of the addiction was marked by the struggle for control; its conclusion, by the loss of control and either abstinence or disaster. One point needs to be very clear: Achieving and maintaining abstinence is *not* controlling your drinking or using. Choosing not to drink or use *at all* means turning the automatism off.

Despite decades of abstinence, the disease, the automatism, is still there. It never goes away; it can only be made dormant.

Clearly, the issue of responsibility is also at the heart of the disease concept of addiction. And here again it is essential to distinguish the *behavior* of drinking or using from the *disease* of addiction.

It is true that a person may be responsible for having placed himself at risk for having developed an addiction by drinking or using drugs in the first place; however, the use of drugs and alcohol is so widespread, so "normal" in our society, that it hardly seems fair to condemn anyone who actually does develop an addiction. Something else must be at work, and precisely why it is that only some people become addicted while others do not is the question of susceptibility (and the subject of chapter 2). For now, let's just say that people *are not* responsible for having an addiction, but that they *are* responsible for dealing with it. And since responsibility depends upon understanding, it follows that a durable understanding is the key to recovery.

THE VALUE OF UNDERSTANDING

Anyone who finds himself at the depths to which an addiction can lead understands very well what it is: something that is going to kill him or otherwise ruin his life if he doesn't do something about it. His understanding doesn't require much thinking. The question that forms the title of this chapter, and to some degree this entire book, is not addressed to the person at that stage of an addiction.

Thinking more critically about addiction is for a different audience: people who have not yet hit some terrible "bottom" and are still bewildered by what they seem unable to control, people who have managed to become abstinent and are faithfully following suggestions (or demands) from others but still don't understand how any of it is going to help, and finally, people who live with or work with alcoholics and addicts in recovery whether those giving the support and counsel have had the experience of addiction themselves or not.

The problem about understanding is that it's made up of two very different elements: what the twentieth-century sage G. I. Gurdjieff called "knowledge" and "being." Often, unfortunately, they are in conflict—education as opposed to experience, an MBA versus "street smarts"—and the development of one at the expense of the other frequently prevents people from helping one another. Thus, the abstinent zealot, experienced in resisting relapse but short on knowledge, who abandons the sober alcoholic who may need to take an antidepressant and, at the other end of the spectrum, the ivory-tower expert whose understanding of addiction is so divorced from reality that his ideas about treatment are not only impractical but even harmful. Understanding requires a balance of knowledge (information) and being (experience).

In the field of addiction treatment, this separation of knowledge and being has created a good deal of mistrust between recovering addicts whose understanding comes largely from experience and those medical, psychological, and counseling professionals whose training has involved mostly receiving information about addiction (reading textbooks, hearing lectures, interviewing patients, and so on). If there is a way of understanding addiction that is both true to experience and also makes sense to people who haven't had one, then a good deal of this mischief may be undone.

The light of this sort of understanding began to dawn in my own mind when I discovered that thousands of people in Alcoholics Anonymous had managed perfectly good recoveries from terrible addictions without having to think much beyond several succinct adages offered them in 12-step meetings (for example, "One day at a time" or "Bring your body; your mind will follow"). That may not seem like much of a discovery to some people, but, for me, it was. And as my understanding grew, I began to suspect that we professionals had been "overthinking" a problem that, for many of the people who had it, wasn't all that complicated.

A LITTLE STORY ABOUT UNDERSTANDING

> If you are the sort of person who cannot understand that when an electrical spark and a spray of atomized petrol meet, there must be an explosion, then perhaps outboard-motor boating is not really a suitable form of recreation for you. Perhaps you should consider golf.
>
> *My imperfect recollection of the introduction to the Seagull*
> *Outboard Motor Company instruction manual, ca.* 1955

For many years, I had the good fortune of sailing a small boat as my main form of outdoor recreation. Common sense dictated having a backup form of getting around in case the wind died or a piece of equipment failed. For me, this meant having an outboard motor, but using it was the last thing I wanted to do. It seemed a capricious and unreliable creature, perversely dying or refusing to start at precisely the worst possible moment. Then, one of my father's old friends found an ancient ¾-hp, single-cylinder job made by the English Seagull Outboard Motor Company and offered it to me, along with the aforementioned instruction manual.

I don't know exactly when it happened, but at some moment after reading the introduction to this little booklet, I understood for the first time that an outboard motor was just a thing, a machine, and that I had completely misunderstood what it was. Without realizing it, and because it worked on its own, I mistook it for a sentient being, a "self" with intelligence and a will of its own. But at that moment, I realized I was being lazy in my mind. Thinking of it that way was nonsense. The thing might be "on," but it had no choice about it. In fact, it was utterly subject to certain laws of nature—primarily, the law of combustion.

If the motor wasn't starting, it wasn't because the motor didn't "want" to start. The motor wasn't starting because the spark and the gas spray weren't meeting. Period. End of discussion. It then became clear to me that "Why won't it start?" was a stupid question or, better put, a question whose answer was already known. The motor wasn't starting because the spark and the gas weren't meeting. Armed with that little bit of understanding, I could then ask the intelligent question: *Why* aren't the gas and the spark meeting? And that, of course, opened the door for all sorts of intelligent actions (the first of which, provided I hadn't simply run out of gas, was to change the spark plug).

It is true that you can cope with many problems reasonably well for a long time by faithfully following a list of instructions: Do this and then do that. But if you understand the essential nature of the thing you're dealing with, you're much better off, because then, when the thing isn't working and you don't have the time or presence of mind to read the instruction manual, you might be able to tap into the creative powers of your mind. A little knowledge may be a dangerous thing but a little understanding, never.

Now, if all this is true for working with an outboard motor, it can't be any less true for dealing with anything else anyone has, including an addiction. So, what is the essential "law" of addiction that yields the same kind of understanding that the law of combustion gives about outboard motors?

POWERLESSNESS: THE ESSENTIAL EXPERIENCE OF ADDICTION

The framers of the American Psychiatric Association's *Diagnostic and Statistical Manual of Mental Disorders* (*DSM*) have also listened carefully to their patients. As a result, they included two criteria for the diagnosis of substance use disorders that are entirely subjective. They can be confirmed only by patients themselves (italics in the following two items are mine):

1. Substance often taken in larger amounts or over a longer period *than the person intended*.

2. A persistent *desire* or one or more unsuccessful *efforts* to cut down or control substance use.

I emphasize these particular words because they exist solely in the *experience* of the addict or alcoholic. No one can judge from observable behavior how seriously the alcoholic *intended* to drink only so much or so long, how much he *desired* to control or cut down his use, or how much *effort* he put into trying to do so. Again, we have to start by accepting that there is something true in what alcoholics and addicts tell us about their experience. When we do, without exception, we hear them report that they have to struggle to control their use of the substance. The longer the struggle goes on, the harder it gets. And in the end control is lost. George Vaillant's findings, detailed in *The Natural History of Alcoholism*, support this point very well. I'll describe the methods of his study fully in chapters 2 and 3. For now, I only want to note that in his staff's interviews with their subjects, one item alone ("Admits problems with control") correctly identified 90 percent of all the alcoholics. It also reliably distinguished them from all those subjects who had some alcohol-related problems but who were not alcoholics.

The people in AA, for whom recovery depends upon sharing experiences with one another, speak of this loss of control as an "allergy of the body and an obsession of the mind." Unfortunately, the idea that alcoholism (or any other addiction) is an allergy has never made much sense to medical professionals.

To us the word *allergy* means a specific immune-system reaction to a foreign substance—hives after eating strawberries or asthma following exposure to cat fur, for example—and no such immune-system response to alcohol has ever been demonstrated. Even Dr. William Silkworth, great friend of the founders of AA and the man who conceived of this formulation, abandoned it later in his career. Still, the idea of an allergy points to a truth: To be an alcoholic means to react to alcohol in an abnormal way. In that sense, alcoholism is like an allergy: a pathological reaction to a substance that is relatively harmless for people without the disorder. It's just that in addiction, the reaction isn't in the immune system but in the central nervous system.

After having a drink or two, a nonalcoholic will have a mildly indifferent (take-it-or-leave-it) attitude about having more. An alcoholic's experience is entirely different. For an alcoholic, having a drink sets off an abnormal reaction, that of wanting more and more to the point of intoxication. As he accumulates the problems that come with frequent intoxication, he begins to struggle to control his use of the substance, a struggle that, over a period of perhaps several years, he will finally lose. Later, we'll consider why those efforts at control are doomed. The point I want to make here is that nonalcoholic drinkers ("normies," as my AA friends call us) simply do not experience this reaction to alcohol. As a result, we do not have to struggle to control our drinking.

So even if an addiction isn't an allergy in the strictly medical sense, the people who have one experience it that way—an abnormal reaction to a substance. Over a period of perhaps many years, something that started out in the realm of choice became involuntary, demanding effort to control and over which control was lost. As it is said in the first step of AA: "We admitted we were powerless over alcohol."

This sense of powerlessness, this experience of losing one's control of one's drinking or use of drugs, however, creates a paradox, the major source of confusion in thinking of addiction as a disease. I call it "the control conundrum."

THE CONTROL CONUNDRUM

Normally, when we think of an illness depriving us of control over some bodily function, we mean going backward, losing control over something we had already acquired. Thus, from a simplistic point of view, the disease of pneumonia results in the loss of effortless breathing, an involuntary function acquired at birth by instinct. In pneumonia, it is said that breathing becomes "labored." Similarly, a stroke deprives one of control over a limb or speech, control that was developed with some effort in growing up. We don't tend to think of these kinds of instinctive functions as having been developed or acquired, but that's only because we can't remember when we didn't have them and we take them for granted.

So here's the puzzle: Whereas alcoholics have the experience of losing control over their drinking, nonalcoholics have no need to control their drinking; they don't have an insatiable desire for more and more. I go to a party. Someone gives me a drink. I have a few sips, then set the glass down as I become involved in conversation. The next thing I know, it's twenty minutes later, and I realize I don't know where my drink is. You can hardly call that kind of moderate drinking being "in control." And even if once in a while I have a bit too much and become a little intoxicated, I don't have the experience of fighting with myself not to have more. I don't want more. I don't particularly like getting drunk. In fact, past a certain point, I definitely dislike it. To an outside observer, someone measuring my drinking behavior, it might look like I'm "in control" of my drinking, but that is certainly not my experience. There is no compulsion that requires me to exert control.

An active alcoholic (meaning "currently drinking") has a completely different experience. After the first drink, he wants more and begins to struggle with himself to keep his drinking within limits. In any particular drinking episode, as he becomes more and more intoxicated, he also becomes less and less capable of exerting that control and, in the end, may well do something stupid, embarrassing, or dangerous. As the results of these episodes accumulate, he begins a campaign to exert control over his drinking: "I'll only drink after five P.M.," or "I'll stay away from hard liquor, only wine or beer," or "I'll only drink with other people, never by myself." But inevitably he violates these self-imposed limits and replaces them with new ones. Now he'll never drink before lunch or only on weekends ... and so it goes. This is the experience of becoming powerless over alcohol.

The great psychologist Mark Twain summed up the futility

of an addict's struggle for control more than one hundred years ago (in speaking of tobacco addiction):

> To cease smoking is the easiest thing I ever did. I ought
> to know because I've done it a thousand times.

Twain's caricature describes an addiction at full maturity: the "all or nothing" end stage that started when urges and thoughts began to have a life of their own. The struggle for control and the ultimate failure to achieve it marks the involuntary essence of addiction and puts it squarely in the category of things we think of as diseases. But what the addict or alcoholic experiences as the *loss* of control is really the result of having *acquired* something that has taken control for itself: an automatism.

AUTOMATICITY: RETHINKING THE DISEASE CONCEPT OF ADDICTION

> **automatism:** *n.* The state or quality of being automatic; the power of self-moving; automatic, mechanical, or involuntary action.
>
> *Webster's New Collegiate Dictionary*

> Mental processes recede from consciousness over time with repeated use . . . [and] become automated, but because we did not start out intending to make them that way . . . we aren't aware of it.
>
> J. A. Bargh and T. L. Chartrand (1999)

> **automatism:** a condition in which an individual is con-
> sciously or unconsciously, but involuntarily, compelled
> to the performance of certain acts, often purposeless
> and sometimes foolish or harmful.
>
> *Stedman's Medical Dictionary,* 21st ed. (1966)

Bicycle riding and swimming are excellent examples of relatively simple automatisms, though of course neither is foolish or
self-destructive. Since they are also common and harmless, they
are especially useful for purposes of discussion; people don't usually have strong opinions about them. I'll use swimming.

As the above definitions indicate, automatisms are involuntary; they "do themselves" in the same way that machines do. We
experience that in two ways: effortlessness and irreversibility.
Really, they are two sides of the same coin.

Although initially learning to swim required effort, once
learned, it never has to be learned again. It has become effortless
in the sense that once you've got it, you don't have to get it again.
It has become automatic. By contrast, learning to speak a foreign
language as an adult requires effort both to acquire and to maintain. Although swimming might become effortful in particular
situations (racing or exercising) or in difficult conditions (against
a current, in cold water, and so on), that's the question of being
able to do it, not of having it. Once swimming has been acquired,
once the automatism has developed, it doesn't have to be learned
again. What once took time to get is now effortlessly, automatically available whenever it is needed.

We experience the irreversibility of an automatism as the
inability to get rid of it, to "unlearn" it, so to speak. Suppose, for

example, that for some reason it became extremely important for you never to swim again (dangerous currents, sharks, motorboats). What choice do you actually have? Since you cannot forget or "unlearn" how to swim, you literally cannot choose *not* to swim. Your only reliable choice is to stay out of the water, to become abstinent. True, a swimmer might try to enjoy the water but avoid swimming by confining himself to the shallows. This would be analogous to the "setting limits" stage of an addiction. It just isn't going to work in the long run. Whether the swimmer intended to or not, if his feet leave the bottom, he'll be swimming again, automatically. As long as he doesn't drift out into the deep water, there may well be no problems, so it won't matter. But that isn't the point. The point is that despite having resolved to stay in the shallows, he is now swimming again.

AAs have a pithy way of describing the irreversibility of an addiction: "You can change a cucumber into a pickle, but you can't turn a pickle into a cucumber." We're all pretty good at distinguishing pickles from cucumbers, but it's not so easy to tell the difference between addicted and nonaddicted alcohol or drug use, the disease from the behavior.

When an addiction is thought of as behavior, we tend to think about it quantitatively rather than qualitatively, to focus on how much or how often a person drinks or uses rather than to listen to what his experience is when he does so. As a result, we miss the essential quality that defines addiction as a disease: Something someone *has* rather than something they're *doing*. Then, just to make things more difficult, alcoholics and addicts themselves, particularly early in the course of their disease, strenuously resist accepting the idea that something is wrong

When their behavior is challenged, they become re-defensive: "I don't drink any more than the other
g out with," or "Everybody at the party was doing the same thing," or "I just have a couple of hits to unwind after work. Is that so terrible?"

By contrast, when the focus is taken off the alcoholic or addict's *behavior* and instead placed on understanding an addiction as an *acquired automatism*, the results can be startlingly different. It's often enough to ask the simple and nonjudgmental question "Have you ever quit drinking (or using) completely?" Then watch the facial response very carefully. A nonalcoholic (a nonaddict) will usually look a little puzzled. Often, he will say something like "Do you mean like giving up wine for Lent or something like that?" *He doesn't really understand the question.* But an addict or alcoholic's face, even if only briefly, will reveal that he understands exactly what you are talking about.

If he's still denying the problem, he'll sometimes launch into a proud recitation of periods of abstinence: "Absolutely! Last year I quit drinking for six months!" Without intending to, he's really telling you that drinking has acquired a life of its own inside him and that he now has to make an effort to control it. As time passes, exerting that control will become more and more difficult, less and less successful. In the end, the only reliable solution will be to give up the effort to control it and to become abstinent.

Again, the automatism of addiction is the distortion in degree or scope of a normal process. A young child, for example, struggles to acquire words and the rules of grammar until he develops the automatism of fluid speech. Only then can he pay attention to a higher level of activity: evaluate whether or not he is actually being understood, reformulate his thoughts, and so on. In fact, without this capacity for automaticity, human beings could not mature into adulthood. But since "every stick has two ends," this otherwise normal characteristic also carries with it the liability of addiction. When drinking or using a drug gets a life of its own and begins to ruin the addict's life, it has become a disease.

Virtually all automatisms have the potential for doing damage in the sense that they deprive us of some freedom of choice. Thus, the humor of the slide I have used in my lectures to illustrate the "loss of control" that comes with the development or acquisition of an automatism:

Don't read this.

Because you have the automatism of reading, you have also "lost control" over it; you cannot choose to look at the statement and do what it says. The experience isn't harmful, of course, and, unlike an addiction, you don't have an irresistible desire to repeat it, but the principle of automaticity is the same. If you want to do what it says, you have to close your eyes or look away. In other words, to disengage the automatism you must abstain, precisely what an alcoholic or drug addict has to do to recover from his loss of control. By contrast, if I had written "*Ne olvasd ezt!*" chances are pretty good you wouldn't have understood what a Hungarian found so amusing; you don't have that automatism. In that case, you would be rather like a normal (nonalcoholic) drinker who doesn't "get" why alcoholics simply don't control themselves better.

Although, in general, we feel justified in taking credit for things that actually now go on by themselves, the truth is that since we like to swim, ride bicycles, and read, we just never think about them in this way. Nevertheless, it remains true that automatisms cannot be unlearned. Once a swimmer, always a swimmer. Or, as it is said in AA, "Once an alcoholic, always an alcoholic."

Why do automatisms develop in response to alcohol and some drugs? For the same reason that swimming or riding a bicycle become automatized: They're important for your survival. The first time you were taken into a swimming pool, your nervous system began coordinating your actions so as not to drown. Over a period of time, all these actions were "crystallized" or "consolidated," one might say, into a single permanent coordinated function called swimming. Then, in order to keep you safe, these actions were made automatic.

The nervous system responds to alcohol and drugs of abuse (if it can) in the same way. The reason is revealed in another old medical expression:

All medicines are poisons.
The secret is in knowing the dosage.

All addictive drugs started out in history as medicines, and, like their nonaddictive cousins, they are also poisons. They affect the highest functions of the central nervous system—our intellectual and emotional intelligence. Hence the street language for intoxication: getting "wasted" or "stupid" or "bombed." As the nervous system strives to compensate for these toxin-induced changes (intoxication), it establishes a state in which these adjustments are automatically activated whenever the substance is taken into the system again. Officially, we call that form of neural adaptation *tolerance*. As tolerance develops, more and more of the substance is needed to produce intoxication.

Alcohol, for example, slows down communication between nerve cells. That's why we like it. I am at dinner with some people I don't know. Initially, I'm a little anxious, but after a glass or two of wine, my brain cells slow down a little, and I relax and enjoy myself and the company more than I might have if I had remained nervous. And although being mildly intoxicated in this way may contribute to my doing or saying something a little embarrassing or foolish, the state itself isn't particularly dangerous. However, if I go on drinking past this state, I become clumsy, uncoordinated, temporarily disabled, and, as a consequence, in danger. If I repeatedly put myself in this dangerous condition, the brain begins to build up tolerance or resistance to the substance in order to protect me.

The brain reacts in a similar way to the opiate family of drugs (morphine, heroin, and their cousins). These substances produce an extraordinary sense of well-being, which is what makes them so valuable in the treatment of acute pain. But this peaceful state of mind is not useful, for example, if, while sitting on the couch loaded, you happen to notice that the curtains have caught fire. In the mental state of "Who cares?" you're just as likely to find the flames fascinating as to put the fire out or get yourself to safety. So, again, the part of the mind concerned with self-preservation recognizes the danger of this state and develops resistance to the effect of these drugs.

The flip side of having developed tolerance to a drug that suppresses brain cell activity is that when the substance is removed, the brain cells "overshoot" the return to normal and produce a very unpleasant and sometimes dangerous withdrawal syndrome. The stimulant drugs produce a different sort of withdrawal. Having been propelled into a state of extra energy, the addict falls into a sluggish and apathetic condition when a drug of this type is withdrawn. In any case, alcoholics and addicts of all types know full well that more of the substance will stop the withdrawal, and they experience this part of the automatism as "craving." In advanced addictions, this craving or drug hunger can be more compelling than almost any other need a human being can experience.

For most people, the negative effects of drinking too much or too often (or of dabbling with one of the opiates or stimulants) are enough to prevent the development of automatized tolerance. But many people who repeatedly become intoxicated do develop such an automatism, just as people who repeatedly go into the water eventually become swimmers. The development of such an automatism means that a line dividing casual use from addiction has been crossed. From that point on, using the drug again inevitably restarts the automatism, and each time that happens, it is reinforced—that is, made more efficiently automatic. As Bargh and Chartrand note, "The process of automation itself is automatic." It's a closed loop the addict experiences as a more and more severe withdrawal syndrome when he stops, and a more and more rapid reinstatement of tolerance when he starts again. As C. S. Lewis's fictional devil, Screwtape, advises his apprentice-nephew Wormwood (on Earth and working on one of us): "An ever increasing craving for an ever diminishing pleasure. That's the formula. It's more certain and it's better *style*. To get the man's soul and give him *nothing* in return—that is what really gladdens our Father's [the Devil's] heart."

Critics of the disease concept of addiction have argued that if addiction were involuntary (or as I'm asserting, automatic), then no one would ever be able to stop drinking or using. Since most alcoholics and addicts do stop at some point in the course of the disorder (even if they subsequently relapse), they contend, then AA's "powerlessness" and the disease concept of alcoholism must be a "myth." In response to the swimming analogy, they would probably argue that swimmers don't keep on swimming automatically until they drown; they choose to stop, to get out of the water. But, of course, one of the consequences of becoming stupefied on drugs and alcohol is that, unlike the swimmer whose mind is not affected by being in the water, the intoxicated addict loses the sense to "get out" before bad things start happening.

As noted, sooner or later most alcoholics and addicts do recognize the harmful consequences of repeated intoxication and, like a tired or frightened swimmer, do quit—at least for a while. What the alcoholic or addict cannot do, however, is return to casual, uncomplicated drinking or using for any significant period of time. Automatisms are irreversible. They cannot be eliminated, but they can be made dormant.

RELAPSE

Relapse, the reawakening of an automatism after a period of dormancy, reveals the involuntary essence of addiction more clearly than anything else. The trouble is that what *becomes* the involuntary experience of having an automatism didn't start out that way. If the addict is in a period of significant abstinence, then a relapse begins as the *choice* to have a drink or use a drug. It's a subtle but important point, and it's easy to miss the transition from voluntary to involuntary because it takes place in the world of the addict's experience, not in his behavior.

In 2007, HBO aired a series on addiction that fell victim to just this error. I knew it the instant I saw the print advertisement. Above the series title *Addiction* was the little phrase "Why can't they just stop?" It may be catchy and, when uttered by an anguished parent or frustrated therapist, unbearably poignant; nevertheless, it isn't the right question, and it set the program off in the wrong direction.

Anyone who has spent much time talking with alcoholics and addicts knows that, as Mark Twain observed, they quit all the time. The problem, again expressed brilliantly in AA, is that they don't "stay quit." This difference between quitting and not starting again isn't mere sophistry; it's critical to understanding what an addiction is and what recovery from addiction really means.

If you think, for example, of addiction as misguided behavior (the "continuing to use a substance despite adverse consequences" definition), then, once the addict stops using, the condition is gone. Alternatively, if you believe the problem is fouled up brain chemistry, then correcting those abnormalities should solve the problem. I've oversimplified these positions, but the huge mass of scientific details connected with them has so obscured the errors inherent in these formulations that it's almost impossible to see the forest for the trees.

The big picture is this: Long after stopping, long after withdrawal and craving have faded, something is still there ready and waiting to be awakened if it's given the opportunity. An addiction never goes away. Even after years of abstinence, the automatism is still there. The solution isn't "just" stopping. The solution is not starting again, and that belongs in the realm of choice, not chemistry.

I can illustrate the dynamics of relapse simply enough with an example from my own struggle with cigarette smoking. I am well aware that tobacco addiction is not the acutely devastating condition that illicit drug or alcohol addiction is, but, for the purposes of this argument, that's so much the better. Using it as an example of the addictive process won't arouse passionate opinions about the addictive personality, bad companions, willpower, moral fiber, and the like. And, anyway, after years of sharing my experience of tobacco addiction with thousands of alcoholics and drug addicts, I am thoroughly convinced that all these experiences are different only in intensity and consequences, not in their essential characteristics. Canaries and eagles are indeed very different, but they are also both birds.

Like Mark Twain (and most smokers), I had quit smoking several times. At one point, I'd even been off cigarettes for about two years. This was a long enough period of time to have forgotten the craving, the cost, the cough, the stinking clothes, and ashes—all the nasty aspects of smoking. Then, at what became the end of this period of abstinence, I took a trip to New York. One evening, my brother-in-law Bob took me out to dinner at one of the most elegant restaurants overlooking the Manhattan skyline. Just before our after-dinner drinks arrived, and much to my surprise, Bob went off to the vending machine to buy some cigarettes.

"Bob, I didn't know you smoked!" I said.

He replied, "Well, you know, just now and then, like tonight, after a great meal and all. It's an occasion! Would you like one?"

Still ignorant of the essence of addiction, I accepted, lit up, and enjoyed again the deep, satisfying hit of a lungful of nicotine. I did not turn instantly into a tobacco-crazed maniac. I did not break into the vending machine, take as much as I could carry, and run away. Far from it. In fact, I had a very nice sense of well-being, the sort of feeling you'd have if you had run into an old friend with whom past difficulties were now forgiven and forgotten. Ten minutes later, I had another. And that was it. No problem. Bob and I finished our drinks and took a cab back to his place for the night.

I slept like a baby until the alarm went off at six A.M. the next day. I stretched, yawned, and with my first breath inhaled the aroma of roasting coffee beans drifting up from the import-export shop on the floor below us.

Is there any reader who cannot guess what the next thought in my head was? Actually, what appeared in my mind wasn't a thought at all. It was an urge, followed by a conversation inside my head that went something like this (AAs call this "the committee"):

"I'd like a cigarette."

"No. I don't want to start the day with a cigarette."

"Don't worry. Just one."

"No, I don't want to get addicted again."

"Relax. You're not going to get addicted from one cigarette."

"OK. I'll have one, but not before breakfast."

Thus resolved to a life of intelligent moderation, I took a shower and ate breakfast. Then, as I looked over the morning paper and began to drink my coffee, the urge to have a cigarette returned, now more insistently. After a brief search failed to turn them up, I turned to Bob.

"Hey, Bob. Where are the cigarettes?"

"What cigarettes?" he replied.

"You know, from last night!"

For a moment, he was puzzled, then said, "Oh, you mean from the restaurant? Gosh, I don't know . . . You know what? I think I may have left them there."

I'd always been fond of Bob, but at that moment . . . Fortunately, my rational mind rescued me from these evil thoughts: It's just as well, I thought, I shouldn't have a cigarette this early in the day anyway. I did decide, however, that if anyone offered me one, I'd feel free to accept. And, of course, it is in just these circumstances that NO ONE offers you a cigarette. So, pretty soon I was compelled to ask for them. That worked for a day or two. Then I took (*stole*, really) a half-empty pack that someone had left on a table. And, by the end of the week, I was buying a carton of my unfiltered brand so as not to run out during the rest of the trip.

What happened? With the first puff, the old automatism was up and running. And, once again, I found myself involuntarily confronted with the urge to have a cigarette, then compelled to think about whether I should do it or not and, if so, when and where and how often and how many, and so on and so forth. It didn't take long to become so tired of this obsessive mental activity that I gave in and went in search of a smoke, if for no other reason than to stop the noise inside my head. But, of course, that lasted only so long, and soon enough I had to have another and then another. . . .

Again, I am not implying that tobacco addiction is as psychologically compelling or acutely damaging as alcohol or drug addiction, but the essential nature of addictions as automatisms and the principle that recovery is founded upon abstinence still holds true. It's only when an addict of any kind really understands that there is no such thing as "just one" that the temptation to have any at all begins to lose its power. Perhaps it's because he's not lying to himself anymore. Again, AA has a marvelous expression for this realization: "One is too many and a thousand not enough."

I finally did stop smoking again in 1983. I claim no heroic achievement. I simply got pneumonia and could hardly breathe for four days, much less smoke. So I went through the worst of the withdrawal relatively easily. And by then I'd talked with about twenty-five hundred alcoholics, and I had begun to understand that their experience with alcohol was the same as my experience with nicotine. For me, there was simply no such thing as "having a cigarette." For me, there was (and still is) either smoking or not smoking and basically nothing in between. I just haven't started up again.

A few years after the pneumonia helped me quit, Bob came to California for a visit. We sailed to Catalina Island and camped out on my boat for several days. The high point after each day's adventure was going to dinner at the restaurant in town and drinking a cocktail while gazing upon the yachts in the harbor and "the States" off in the distance. Naturally, Bob bought a pack of cigarettes and then offered me one.

Now in past periods of abstinence, while refusing a cigarette, a little voice in my head would have commented, "I don't want a cigarette. I don't like smoking. Cigarettes are bad for me." All of which, at that point, really wasn't true. I *did* want a cigarette. I *did* like smoking. *One* cigarette wouldn't hurt me. But by that point, I also understood the larger, more important truth: I am a tobacco addict. So for me, it wouldn't be one cigarette. Soon enough, I would be smoking again.

The real question I had to ask myself was whether or not I wanted to go down that road, because that's what was going to happen. Once again I'd get tired of fighting the urge, tired of fighting to control my thinking, and once again I'd give in. Since I didn't (and still don't) want to die of emphysema or lung cancer if there is any way for me to avoid it, I politely refused and, amazingly, didn't crave it. Twenty-five years later, I still don't.

Bob, who, for unfathomable reasons, has never been addicted to cigarettes, can have one now and then. I don't know why. I only know I can't. No one is to blame. It's just how it is: as when an electrical spark and a spray of atomized petrol meet.

PROGRESSION

Finally, in order to round out this understanding of the disease concept of addiction, it's necessary to speak about one more feature addictions share with other diseases. It's what we speak of in medicine as the "course" of an illness or its "progression," and it brings up yet one more paradox: Addictions both do and do not progress. It's rather like pregnancy: From one point of view, pregnancy is a state. There is no such thing as being "kind of" pregnant; a woman either is or is not pregnant. At the same time, the course of a pregnancy isn't an all-or-nothing state; there's a big difference between being six weeks or nine months along.

It's the same with addictions. At some point a threshold is crossed, a corner is turned. You may not have had the automatism before that moment, but now you do, and, as with all other automatisms, there's no going back. It's a state that, like pregnancy, is either present or not. But, just as a pregnancy develops, so too the consequences of having an addiction progress. What that progression will look like (that is, what kinds of consequences result from it) will have as much to do with social and psychological factors as it will with the physical and psychological effects of the particular drug.

Nicotine, at least for some people, may well be as physically addicting a drug as heroin, but because it's legal and not nearly so rapidly debilitating, the consequences of becoming addicted to it are not so severe, at least in the short run. Tobacco addicts don't get arrested for stealing and prostituting, don't get AIDS or hepatitis, don't overdose, and so on.

By contrast, and although it too eventually creates a powerful craving, alcohol addiction has consequences that have nothing to do with its legal status: As the addiction progresses, more and more of the alcoholic's internal organs are damaged or destroyed. So, in this case, the progression of the disease is far more a matter of biology than a result of the legality of the drug. And again, cocaine or amphetamine addiction progress in a manner dictated by yet a different combination of psychological, social, and biological factors.

It has become commonplace to speak of addiction, as it was put in the HBO special, as a "chronic, relapsing brain disease." Dr. Steven Hyman, writing in the *American Journal of Psychiatry* on the occasion of the thirtieth anniversary of the founding of the National Institute of Drug Abuse, called addiction "a recalcitrant, chronic and relapsing condition." Unfortunately, these formulations of the disease concept of addiction contain a subtle error and are unintentionally misleading. Multiple sclerosis is a chronic, relapsing brain disease. No matter what anyone does (or doesn't do) about it, the neurological deterioration in MS is relentless in its course. At present there is no known way to stop it. Addictions are simply not that kind of disease. Addictions don't relapse. People relapse.

Opponents of the disease concept of addiction are correct in exposing the error of thinking that alcoholics and drug addicts are utterly ruled by uncontrollable brain chemistry. Relapse is not inevitable. Addicts can choose to stop and stay stopped. But let's not throw the disease-concept baby out with the helpless-victim bathwater. Just because addicts can choose to stop doesn't mean they chose to have the addiction in the first place.

This distinction between what is and isn't involuntary about addiction is the same as that in other illnesses where progression can be arrested. A diabetic doesn't choose to have the disease, but if he eats without restraint and neglects to take his medication regularly, the disease spins out of control and causes all sorts of physical problems. In the same way, if an addict doesn't stay abstinent, then the consequences of his addiction get more and more serious. In both cases, the individual hasn't chosen to have the disease; he only chooses whether or not to treat it.

If there is anything unique about the disease of addiction, it is the extent to which the really critical part of treatment is in the hands of the patient. Over and over again, "one day at a time," alcoholics and addicts must *choose* to abstain in order to maintain recovery. To argue, as opponents of the disease concept do, that because people can make that choice, addiction is not a disease is to disregard the experience of millions of people. On the other hand, suggesting, as the brain scientists do, that an addiction relapses on its own, betrays a misunderstanding of the essential nature of the disorder. Both errors miss the real source of recovery.

Sadly, the misconception of addiction as a "chronic, relapsing disease" reflects a much larger failure of the modern medical model: a growing disregard of the person who has a disease in favor of knowing more and more about the biochemical and physiological mechanisms of the disease itself. As a result, the scientifically based medical community increasingly regards all patients, including addicts and alcoholics, as passive carriers of problematic parts that we, the treatment professionals, are obligated to try to "fix" with a medication or some other technique. The HBO special, for example, which relied heavily on academic and institutionally based experts, devoted a whole segment to three medications that have only marginal value in long-term recovery from alcoholism, while at the same time making almost no mention of Alcoholics Anonymous and the other 12-step groups.

The "fix-it" approach may work for some illnesses, but, as will be seen, it is an unmitigated disaster in the treatment of addiction. We will never have a "cure" for addiction as we do, say, for an infectious disease like pneumonia. In fact, given the essential nature of addiction, the very idea of a "cure"—a treatment the addict could receive passively—is absurd. I'll have a good deal more to say about this in chapters 3 and 4, because it bears on the difference between mere abstinence and true recovery. Abstinence, though necessary, is simply self-denial. Recovery, on the other hand, is the affirmation of a life wisdom that brings the abstinent alcoholic or addict to a place where he no longer *wants* to become intoxicated, no matter what life throws at him. But more of this later.

SUMMING UP

To conclude this chapter, let me state as simply as I can why and how we should consider addiction a disease.

1. An addiction is something people have, not something they are doing. Addictions are manifested in behavior, but they are not the behavior itself.

2. Like all other diseases, addictions are harmful, abnormal, and involuntary.

3. The essential involuntary quality of an addiction is that of powerlessness, of "losing control": the experience of involuntary desires (craving), unwanted thoughts (obsession), and conflicted actions (compulsion).

4. The loss of control in an addiction is the consequence of having developed an automatism. Addictions, therefore, are disorders of automaticity.

5. Automatisms are permanent acquisitions. They can be made dormant, but they cannot be eliminated.

6. Since automatisms cannot be eliminated, the progressive harm they cause can be arrested only by abstinence.

7. Relapse is the reawakening of an automatism after a period of dormancy.

A final final note: After considerable searching, I found my old copy of the Seagull instruction manual but could not find the introductory paragraph I thought I remembered. Even so, the *spirit* of the manual is very well expressed in what I dreamed up. I hope I may be forgiven the fiction.

Chapter Two

WHY ME?

People often react to bad medical news with the question "Why me?" All too often, what they really mean is "What did I do to deserve this?" As if getting sick were punishment for something they'd done. Asked in this way, the question is a protest, a holdover from childhood, and understandable. The trouble is that it obscures a really good question: Why *does* one person get sick, while another does not? In any given year, between 60 and 70 percent of all adult Americans will be exposed to alcohol, but only a fraction of them are alcoholics. Why some and not all? Why you and not me? Or vice versa?

The answer to this question is not simple. Even so, thinking in this area has become unnecessarily muddled because medical science hasn't had a unifying concept of addiction as a disease. When addictions are defined as behaviors, it makes sense to ask, for example, why John drinks "excessively" and Mary doesn't. The trouble with this approach, as I hope I have shown in the previous chapter, is that drinking, excessive or otherwise, is not alcoholism. Moreover, trying to figure out why anyone does anything, if pursued seriously, reveals that what can be reduced by someone else to observable behavior, might well be experienced by the subject himself as a confusing mass of contradictory motives. In the study of addiction, frustration with this kind of complexity has led to all kinds of simplistic formulations that are held to explain "the" cause. The one that makes me particularly crazy is "alcoholism is hereditary."

Let's at least start with the right question. The question isn't what causes John or Mary to drink or use this or that much, this or that often. The question is, if both John and Mary have been exposed to alcohol, then why has John developed the automatism—the addiction—and Mary has not? It may be possible to describe the essence of addiction simply, but, alas, there is no simple answer as to what causes it. The same is true of many other diseases.

An addiction, like any other disease, is the result of the coming together of three factors: an agent of harm, a host, and the host's reaction to that agent. In medical shorthand, we call that combination *resistance* and its inverse *susceptibility*.

RESISTANCE AND SUSCEPTIBILITY

Once again, the medical profession itself is responsible for some of the simplistic cause-and-effect thinking about diseases. Beginning in the 1880s, when the germ theory was first winning acceptance, a kind of enthusiastic innocence captured the medical imagination. Illnesses that had defied centuries of medical practice were discovered to be associated with newly recognized microorganisms. Who can blame physicians for thinking of these infectious agents as "the" cause of this or that disease? After thousands of years of helpless frustration, they finally began to see the promise of fighting diseases effectively. It must have been a heady time. The actual discovery of "magic bullets"—specific chemicals capable of selectively killing the offending germ—reinforced the impression of cause and effect: Kill the germ, cure the disease.

This approach worked so well (and still does) for so many infections that we have tended to forget the body's role in fighting off agents of harm. The AIDS epidemic and the emergence of some really frightening, antibiotic-resistant germs (e.g., TB) have reawakened some forgotten truths about susceptibility, resistance, and disease. Some germs are so virulent that virtually everyone who is exposed gets sick, but that isn't the case for all germs. The same is true for intoxicating drugs thought of as agents of harm. Unless everyone who is exposed to a particular intoxicating substance develops an addiction to it, then there must be additional factors at work, factors that either protect you or make you more susceptible. Agents of harm, then, whether they are germs or chemicals, are *necessary* but not *sufficient* causes of illnesses. The disease known commonly as "strep throat" provides a good example of this concept.

The agent of harm in this disease is the bacterium *Streptococcus*. But at any given moment, a significant proportion of healthy schoolchildren have this very germ living in their throats. They aren't sick because their resistance holds the growth of the germs in check. So developing the actual infection requires more than simply having the agent of harm; the child must also lose resistance to that agent. Many different factors play a role in the loss of resistance: heredity, nutrition, other illnesses, stress, and so on. In addition, our resistance changes as we age. The virus that causes an inconvenient cold when you're twenty can kill you at seventy.

The same principle applies to alcoholism and drug addiction. Think of the chemicals themselves (alcohol, opiates, stimulants, etc.) as very simple germs that require a host to come to life. In the "agent-host-resistance" scheme for alcoholism, the agent of harm is alcohol. The condition it produces is an addiction, an automatism. Just as in the example of strep throat, many more people are exposed to this agent of harm than become ill from it. So, at the risk of oversimplifying, there must be factors influencing susceptibility to developing an addiction.

The rest of this chapter explores some specific answers to the "Why me?" question. Again, I want to acknowledge a somewhat delicate wording. I am not saying that such and such is "the" cause of addiction. What I am saying is that there are several different kinds of factors that influence our resistance and therefore our susceptibility to developing an addiction. Perhaps that's a bit wordy, but it's the only way of getting at "Why me?" as a serious question rather than a complaint.

RISK FACTORS FOR DEVELOPING
AN ADDICTION

The famous story of the blind men and the elephant (at least the version I know) seems a good place to begin talking about the difficulties of establishing what factors put people at risk for the development of an addiction.

Once upon a time there was a king who had his wise men working on the creation of an encyclopedia. He'd heard reports of a fabulous creature in India called an elephant and wanted to include it in his book. So, he gathered three of his wise men together and said, "Go find an elephant. If you can bring it back, do so, but if you cannot, prepare a report for the encyclopedia. I will give twenty pieces of silver to the one who writes the best report."

Now in those days all wise men were blind. I don't know why, but it was so. Today, wise men have to have several degrees after their names, but in those days wise men had to be blind.

In time, the wise men did indeed find an elephant. The first wise man ran into the animal's side. He realized immediately that he couldn't bring the creature back, so he set about writing his report, which he entitled "How the Elephant Is Like a Wall." The second blind wise man encountered one of the elephant's legs, also realized he'd have to write a report, and entitled his treatise "How the Elephant Resembles a Tree Trunk." The third wrote a report called "How the Elephant Is Like a Snake Suspended from the Sky." You can guess what he got hold of.

Now, each of the wise men was so eager to receive the reward that he concealed his report from the others and spoke only in generalities and with false humility.

The king, upon receiving these three completely different reports concluded that his wise men were either mad, incompetent, or deceitful. He had them all executed, and the elephant never did make it into the encyclopedia.

The elephant, of course, is addiction. The three blind wise men are biologists, sociologists, and psychologists. Scientists working in each of these disciplines are "blind" and unable to cooperate, partly out of ambition and the pressures of academic life but, more important, as a result of extreme specialization. As a result of knowing more and more about less and less, it has become almost impossible for different specialists to understand, let alone appreciate, one another's work. The consequence is that many addiction researchers are relatively ignorant of the significance of work done by their colleagues in other disciplines. And, in the end, that means that fewer and fewer people have the kind of perspective that could lead to an understanding of the big picture.

And that's not the least of it. As instructive as the elephant story may be, it's an imperfect analogy. Compared with addiction researchers, the king's wise men had it easy; at least the elephant was fully formed by the time they ran into it. By contrast, addictions can take years to develop. At some point, an addiction does become the unmistakable automatism I described in chapter 1, but before that point it can be very difficult to distinguish problematic drug or alcohol use from what, for some, will go on to become the full-blown disorder. It's as though the elephant resembled a rhino when it was a baby, a hippo in its teen years, and then finally in adulthood what we all recognize as an elephant. Since the vast majority of studies exploring the causes of addiction are *retrospective*, they examine the elephant only *after* it became one. Had they followed the creature from childhood, so to speak, they might have come up with very different conclusions.

Much of my own effort to think simply about the causes of addiction is taken directly from George Vaillant's great study, *The Natural History of Alcoholism*, published in 1983. It is a brilliant book on a very complicated subject, and, although it is wonderfully organized and beautifully written, it is also very difficult—so much so—that it is unlikely that anyone who isn't taking a course on addiction or psychology will read it. That's my justification for the fact that much of this chapter is based on it.

What makes Vaillant's study so important is that, unlike almost all other large-scale studies of alcoholism (or any other addiction), it is *prospective*: It follows subjects into the future before they have (or have not) become alcoholics. Again, by contrast, *retrospective* studies start with subjects who are already in trouble with alcohol. To extend the elephant analogy a little, it is as though one wise man understood that sometimes what looks like it might become an elephant doesn't. Ten or twenty years on, you discover that it actually became a hippo, a whole different category for the encyclopedia and much less confusion for the king.

The study itself began in about 1940 with two fairly large groups of subjects. The first, referred to as the "Core City" group, came from working-class neighborhoods in Boston, numbered about four hundred, and were selected for the study in the late 1930s when they were junior high school students. The second group was composed of two hundred men selected as sophomores in college (originally as part of a study in normal adult development). In both instances, none of the subjects were alcoholic *at the time* they were entered in the study. A third group of subjects, added later, was followed forward for eight years after they went through treatment. All this means, first of all, is that all the "chicken-or-egg" questions that have bedeviled addiction research since the beginning of time can be examined. Put simplistically, one of those questions might go like this: Did the man become an alcoholic because he was depressed? Or did he become depressed after he became an alcoholic? Retrospective studies cannot answer such questions reliably.

Over the first forty years of the study (subsequent updates have appeared in journal articles), the men in the first two groups had frequent and detailed psychiatric evaluations and repeated physical exams. Relatives were interviewed. Medical, court, and employment records were examined and so on. All kinds of things had happened to them by 1980, when the data were first analyzed, but of particular interest to Vaillant and his colleagues was that at some point, about a quarter of the men in the Core City group of four hundred met criteria for either alcohol abuse or dependence (alcoholism).

Since all the subjects were selected for the study before they'd developed alcoholism, the researchers had an unprecedented opportunity to ask all kinds of questions that might shed some light on why some people become alcoholics and others do not. The study does, of course, have some limitations—the subjects were all men and mostly from one geographical area—but these problems pale in comparison to the richness of the data the study has provided.

In summary, here are some of the factors that did *not* predict whether any particular subject was going to become an alcoholic: low IQ, parents in a low socioeconomic class, high boyhood competence, growing up in a multiproblem family, childhood emotional problems, inadequate maternal supervision, and warm relationship with mother. Some of the factors that were associated with future alcoholism were: Irish ethnicity, alcoholism in family background, school behavior problems, lack of a cohesive family, lack of childhood environmental strengths, less than a tenth-grade education, and two or more times in jail.

These factors, however, are still only correlations. Alcoholism occurred more frequently when these factors were present early in a subject's life. Correlations hint at causality, but they don't prove it.

In trying to simplify how different factors contribute to the risk of developing alcoholism or drug addiction, I have found the following outline useful. It isn't intended to be exhaustive, and I will touch only briefly on each type of factor in the text.

My aim is to keep a sense of the big picture and not get lost in the details.

RISK FACTORS FOR DEVELOPING AN ADDICTION

I. Biological Factors
    A. Genetic factors
        1. studies of adoptees
        2. studies of twins
        3. *The Natural History of Alcoholism*
    B. Acquired biological factors ("addictiveness")
        1. different substances
        2. different methods of use

II. Sociological Factors
    A. Availability: the contagious-disease model
    B. Social conditions
    C. Cultural expectations: peer pressure, advertising

III. Psychological Factors
    A. Mental illness
    B. Personality

BIOLOGICAL FACTORS

By "biological factors" I mean the sorts of things that affect susceptibility to developing an addiction on a purely physical basis, known or unknown biochemical and structural elements of our bodies. Some of these factors are inherited, but others are acquired later in life and may be more apt to lead to addiction because of the nature of the substance itself rather than anything specific to the person using it. A few examples of both will make the point.

GENETIC FACTORS

Studies of Adoptees

It has been known for a long time that alcoholism runs in families. For the most part, this has never been regarded as particularly surprising; after all, speaking French also runs in families. Both are learned, aren't they? In 1974, the psychiatrist Donald Goodwin and his team conducted some landmark investigations designed to answer just this question. His book *Is Alcoholism Hereditary?* is excellent, except, in my opinion, for its title, because the proper answer to the question posed is no. If the title had been the unwieldy *Are There Hereditary Factors in Alcoholism?* the answer would have been a resounding yes. In any case, it is a very important study.

Goodwin and his colleagues went to Denmark (officials there have kept excellent records of this kind) to examine rates of alcoholism in the families of people who'd been adopted very early in life. At the time of the study, all of the adoptees were adults. A number were determined to be alcoholics and were matched with a control group made up of patients in an outpatient psychiatric clinic (i.e., people who had emotional problems but were not alcoholic).

The idea behind the study was that all adoptees have two families: their adoptive family, from whom they have learned things (like language), and their biological family, from whom they inherited things (like eye color). If alcoholism runs in families because it is learned, then the researchers should have found more alcoholism in the adoptive parents of the children who later developed alcoholism themselves. If, on the other hand, there are genetic factors at work in alcoholism, then there should be more alcoholism in the biological parents of the adoptees who later became alcoholics.

In summary, Goodwin and his colleagues found that the rate of alcoholism in the *biological* parents of the adoptees who later became alcoholics themselves was four times greater than that for the adoptees who did not become alcoholics. Here's another, perhaps simpler way of putting it: If one of your biological parents was an alcoholic, you have a four times increased risk of becoming an alcoholic yourself even if you are adopted and grow up in another family where there is no alcoholism.

The study also showed that there was no significant difference between the frequency of alcoholism in the *adoptive* families of the children who later became alcoholics and those who did not. So, if your biological parents were not alcoholics but you were adopted into a family where there was an alcoholic parent, your risk of developing alcoholism is no greater than if you'd grown up in a nonalcoholic household. That's very strong evidence that something genetic is influencing the development of alcoholism.

Studies of Twins

Comparing alcoholism rates in identical and fraternal twins has provided excellent additional evidence of the involvement of genetic hereditary factors in the development of alcoholism. Identical twins share essentially the same heredity because they both came from the same egg and sperm set. Fraternal twins, on the other hand, just happen to be born at the same time; they come from two different sets of egg and sperm and are no more (or less) genetically similar than other siblings born at different times.

Both kinds of twins, however, have some important common factors, factors that might be important in the development of an addiction. Although family problems (and strengths) might well affect each member of a twin pair somewhat differently, at least they are the same events, and they happen at the same time in the twins' lives. Perhaps, for example, losing a parent at age nine or moving frequently increases the risk of developing alcoholism later on in life. These are the kinds of factors that would be the same for each member of a twin set, whether they are fraternal or identical. What is dramatically different about these twin sets, however, is the amount of heredity they share. It's certainly not a perfect way of separating the effects of "nature" (genetics) from "nurture" (environment), but it's an approach nevertheless.

The differences between these kinds of twin sets are studied by examining concordance rates (*concord* meaning "agreement"). In other words, if one of the twins is an alcoholic, what is the likelihood that the other twin is also? Although the numbers from these kinds of studies have varied somewhat, the trend is clear: Identical twins have about twice the concordance rate for alcoholism—50 percent "alikeness"—compared to only 25 percent for fraternal twins.

Permit me to repeat: *Alcoholism is not hereditary*. If alcoholism were determined by hereditary factors alone, there would be a 100 percent concordance rate for the identical twins. What the evidence from these twin studies does allow us to state is that, at least for some people, there are hereditary factors that contribute to the risk of developing alcoholism.

The Natural History of Alcoholism

I'd like to refer again to Vaillant's great study, *The Natural History of Alcoholism*, because it confirms that heredity plays a significant role in susceptibility to alcoholism. One hundred and seventy-eight of the four hundred Core City subjects had no relatives with a history of alcoholism. Of this group, only 10 percent became alcoholic. But of the seventy-one men who did have a family history of alcoholism, 34 percent went on to develop alcoholism themselves. The same percentage difference was found in the college sample. So, if there was alcoholism in the man's family, he had a three times increased risk of becoming an alcoholic himself.

What these genetic factors may be is a topic of intense research just now, but as yet there have been no definitive answers. It must also be said that we simply do not know whether or not these same findings hold true for susceptibility to other addictive substances (cocaine, heroin, nicotine, etc.). It's almost impossible to do prospective research on the people who use them.

ACQUIRED BIOLOGICAL FACTORS
(THE "ADDICTIVENESS" OF A DRUG)

Different Substances

Acquired biological factors have to do with the fact that only certain substances elicit the addictive response in human beings. With most of these substances, the development of an addiction begins with tolerance to the drug: As time passes, it takes more and more of the drug to produce intoxication. As this tolerance develops, the addict also develops a characteristic withdrawal syndrome if he stops the drug abruptly. An oft-quoted expression describes this progression neatly:

> First the man takes a drink;
> then the drink takes a drink;
> then the drink takes the man.

The alcoholic's withdrawal tremors of the day after are remarkably effective in undoing the previous night's resolve to quit. Almost every cocaine addict I have ever talked with described beginning a binge with the firm intention of smoking only "a little," and then, propelled by the dysphoria of "coming down" from the first hit, scrambling to the ATM to pay for another and another. An acquired biological factor has to do with the power inherent in any particular drug to induce the addictive response. Some drugs, like inhaled nicotine or cocaine, are addictive for almost everyone, whereas other drugs (i.e., alcohol) are significantly weaker.

Not only is there a difference in the power of these substances to produce intoxication and tolerance, but there may also be individual differences in the kind of drug to which each particular person is likely to become addicted. I have had many patients who, despite having been heavily involved in cocaine use, didn't care for the effects of alcohol, and vice versa. It's the same for the hallucinogens and opiates. Clearly, if a particular drug doesn't "work" for you, your chances of becoming addicted to it are diminished.

Different Methods of Use

Different methods of using the same drug can also dramatically change its addictive power. Hundreds of patients have told me the same story illustrating this point with respect to cocaine. As long as they were snorting the drug, they had no sense of being "out of control," but when they began injecting it intravenously or, more commonly, smoking it in the form of "freebase" or "crack," then addiction followed rapidly. This is a classic example of an acquired biological factor (i.e., not a biological factor you were born with), and there is a relatively straightforward explanation for this change in the drug's addictive potential. When cocaine is snorted or rubbed on mucous membranes, it takes about 2.5 minutes to reach peak blood levels. When smoked, it takes only 8.5 seconds. The faster the climb in blood level the more intense the "high." The more intense the high, the more intense the associations that attach to it—associations that will later trigger intense cravings. Something like a variation of the law of gravity applies here. It isn't just that "what goes up must come down." In this case, the faster it goes up, the faster it comes down, and this rapid fall in cocaine blood levels triggers a more intense craving than the more gradual fall in blood level that follows snorting it. In the end, all this makes smoking cocaine more addictive than any other way of using it.

SOCIOLOGICAL FACTORS

Sociologists study people insofar as they are members of one or another group. From the perspective of a strictly medical model, social factors don't tell us much about why a particular individual's resistance was overwhelmed by an agent of harm and another person's was not. Both may be part of the same group—impoverished or unemployed, Hispanic or Anglo, for example—and yet one becomes addicted and the other does not. At the same time, some of the greatest advances in modern medicine have been the result of treating large populations of people rather than individuals. Large-scale public-health measures like sanitary drinking water and mass immunizations are good examples. To some extent, addictive illnesses can be examined in the same way, as though these chemicals were germs and the illnesses they caused were epidemics. From this perspective, there are at least three broad areas that influence susceptibility to developing an addiction: availability, social conditions, and cultural expectations.

Availability

The recent history of cocaine use provides an excellent example of the contagious-disease model as it applies to addictive disorders. I witnessed a little bit of this history personally. Of the roughly three hundred patients I hospitalized for addiction problems in 1980, perhaps a dozen or so were addicted to cocaine. There just wasn't that much cocaine around then, and what was available was hard to get and expensive.

Sometime in the early 1980s, however, two things happened. First, users discovered an easy way to convert cocaine salt to "freebase" cocaine and a little later to "crack," much more potent forms of the same drug (because they could be smoked). Second, there came the South American cocaine cartels, which grew, processed, and distributed the cocaine salt. These groups took over the market as well as increasing demand by lowering the price, a classic business strategy for success. The result was that by 1989, both the availability and the addictiveness of cocaine had increased tremendously. In that year, about half of the patients entering my hospital's addiction treatment program were there for cocaine addiction.

This scenario is only the latest in the long history of addictive substances. The first epidemics of alcoholism, for example, followed the mass production (increased availability) of English gin (a more concentrated form of alcohol than beer or ale). In contrast to all this, there is very little alcoholism in strictly Islamic nations, for the simple reason that alcohol is essentially unavailable. The drug that is widely available, opium, causes plenty of addiction problems (particularly now in Afghanistan).

SOCIAL CONDITIONS

As with many other illnesses, the debilitating effects of addictions are much more severe among the poor and socially dispossessed. There may be an equal amount of alcohol and drug addiction across all socioeconomic groups, but the affluent are much better protected from the consequences of addiction because they have access to decent housing, good nutrition, legal representation, and timely medical care.

It is well known, on the other hand, that the vicious cycles of poverty, unemployment, and welfare dependence both feed and are fueled by addiction to drugs and alcohol. Addicts and alcoholics are notoriously unreliable partners for anything, and repeatedly being fired, hospitalized, or incarcerated doesn't make you any more attractive to a potential employer or mate. That, in turn, further demoralizes people and provides more incentive to escape through intoxication.

Additional social conditions (that is, other than strictly economic) undoubtedly contribute to the incidence of alcoholism and drug addiction. One wonders, for example, whether the apparently high rates of alcoholism in the formerly Communist nations of Eastern Europe and Russia aren't partly a result of the sense of individual futility that came with living in a totalitarian state.

CULTURAL EXPECTATIONS

Different cultural groups have very different expectations when it comes to drinking and drug-using behavior, and these cultural factors play a significant role in the appearance and consequences of addictive disorders. Vaillant points out that in France and Italy, for example, drinking wine at meals is normal, expectable behavior. Children are not only permitted but encouraged to drink wine from a very young age. On the other hand, "out-of-control" drinking—making a spectacle of oneself as the result of public intoxication—is very much disapproved of in Italy but not so much in France. France has a far higher rate of alcoholism.

Drinking practices in other European cultures are different still. In Ireland, for example, there is virtually no drinking at meals, and what drinking does go on is none of the children's business. Gross intoxication in a public setting may not be overtly expected of men (though it may be, particularly after the work week is over), but it doesn't set one apart as unacceptably different.

Perhaps as a result of these different expectations, both rates of alcoholism and its consequences are different in different cultures. In France, for example, there is a high incidence of the physical damage that results from heavy drinking (especially cirrhosis of the liver), while in Ireland, social damage (physical abuse, family dysfunction, incarceration) resulting from alcoholism predominates. To some degree these are oversimplifications, but they do reflect the point about the possible effects of cultural expectations. I say "possible" because heredity and culture are closely intertwined, and the roles played by each in susceptibility to alcoholism have to be teased apart.

The Natural History of Alcoholism is again helpful here because it's based on data that was first gathered in the early 1940s, a time when ethnic and cultural influences were still a powerful factor in people's lives. Neighborhoods were often ethnically distinct, and many of the people in them were either first-generation American or the original immigrants themselves. This was certainly true of the Bostonians who became Vaillant's subjects, and that made it possible to ask the kinds of questions that can separate the roles of culture and genes in susceptibility to alcoholism.

In brief, men of Irish descent had a far higher rate of alcoholism than their counterparts who came from Italian families. That fact alone doesn't answer the question; it could still be genetics at work. What comes much closer to answering it was finding that a man of Italian descent who had many alcoholic relatives was five times more likely to become an alcoholic himself than a man who came from an Italian family that had no history of alcoholism. But still, this only almost answers the question; maybe growing up with many alcoholic relatives overrules what the culture tries to instill. Vaillant was able to address this question as well: Of fifty-one men who had a generally healthy childhood environment, even though it included an alcoholic parent, 27 percent became alcoholics; of fifty-six men with an unsupportive childhood environment but no alcoholic parent, only 5 percent became alcoholic. So, though both probably play a role in susceptibility to alcoholism, it would appear that heredity trumps culture.

It is now nearly seventy years since Vaillant's data were first collected, and the old ethnic neighborhoods on which it was based have vanished. And, in any case, after only a few generations in "the great melting pot," most Americans have abandoned the cultural expectations of their immigrant grand-parents in favor of mainstream American values, values now communicated almost instantly to millions and increasingly dominated by commercial interests. From what I've seen, it would appear that greed, lust, and vanity still have terrific selling power.

Apart from this virtual community, the actual communities we inhabit are fragmented: Groups form around work, family, or school and then disperse. Many have little or nothing in common, and what's acceptable in one group can be entirely unacceptable in another. More than perhaps ever before, people are torn by conflicting roles (*stressed* seems to be the going word) and so are at greater risk to try to rid themselves of that discomfort with alcohol or drugs.

PSYCHOLOGICAL FACTORS

The question of psychological factors influencing susceptibility to addiction is one of the most controversial in the field. Boiled down, it takes two forms:

1. What is the relation between addictions and psychological problems?
2. Is there an addictive personality?

It takes no special genius to note that addicts and alcoholics are troubled people. The tough question is which came first? Do people become addicted because they have emotional problems, or does becoming addicted lead to serious psychological problems? Of course, the question is oversimplified, and so the correct, if unhelpful, answer is yes.

MENTAL ILLNESS

On the one hand, it is well known that people with all kinds of psychiatric disorders are at high risk for developing a substance use problem or outright addiction. Depressed patients may discover, for example, that a stimulant or an opiate gives them a temporary lift or that alcohol helps them get to sleep. People with severe anxiety or phobias (irrational fears) find that alcohol calms them down enough to go about their business—at least, for a while. There are many more examples. Unfortunately, these attempts at self-medication are self-defeating in the long run, and, in the end, the patient winds up with two problems: the original psychiatric disorder and an addiction, to boot.

On the other hand, it is not correct to conclude that all addicts and alcoholics, even those who present with psychiatric symptoms, had a preexisting or underlying psychiatric condition. The consequences of having an addiction are quite sufficient to make anyone miserable. If the brain's chemical roller-coaster ride on repeated episodes of intoxication weren't depressing enough, then all the things that happen to people who become addicted—the lost jobs, ruined relationships, and multiple medical problems—will certainly make up the difference.

For an individual patient, the question of which came first, the addiction or the psychiatric disorder, is sometimes impossible to unravel (and especially not quickly). In such a case, the best thing is for the patient to become entirely drug free, including, *if possible*, from prescribed psychoactive drugs (antidepressants, stimulants, and antianxiety agents) for as long as symptoms permit, and for physician and patient both to wait to see what happens. Many times, what was thought to be an underlying psychiatric problem turns out to be a result of the addiction.

On the other hand, there may well be underlying psychiatric disorders that do not improve with sobriety alone. Many of these problems may get worse if medical treatment is withheld. It is then important for physician and patient alike to acknowledge the benefits of abstinence (and of a recovery program) in addition to the value of appropriate psychiatric treatment. I know I am making this sound simple; it is not. Such a balance between recovery and psychiatric treatment requires all the skill and patience a treatment professional may have.

PERSONALITY

The question of the "addictive personality" is also a matter of serious controversy. Does it exist? If so, what is it?

First, some clarification is in order. If by the word *personality* we mean simply the way people are behaving *now*, at this particular moment (or in the relatively recent past), then it is true that addicts and alcoholics act in characteristic ways. Being intoxicated and doing whatever it takes to get and use drugs or alcohol means sacrificing something or someone else. As a result, the addict becomes less and less concerned with the needs of the other people in his life—friends, family, employer, neighbors—and more and more concerned with himself. This excessive self-centeredness resembles the narcissistic personality disorder, a pattern of behavior and attitudes in which the person demands attention from others in order to prop up a damaged sense of self. The addict also has more tangible problems that get him into trouble and for which he demands support: to be bailed out of jail, to have his rent paid, and so on. If he is still denying his addiction, he fails to see what caused the problems in the first place, and when his behavior is challenged, he falls back on the defense mechanisms we all learned as children and which narcissists never grow out of: blame, projection, and denial.

> BLAME: "If you would quit nagging me all the time, I
> wouldn't have to drink!"
> PROJECTION: "You have your glass of wine every
> night! Who are you to tell me not to drink?
> DENIAL: "I wasn't drinking. Maybe you're smelling
> my mouthwash or something."

Narcissism of this kind, and the defenses that maintain it, especially in the context of an addictive disorder, may or may not reflect the deeper, lifelong kinds of characteristics that define what professionals usually mean by the word *personality*. My friend and colleague Dr. Timmen Cermak calls it "the acquired narcissistic personality disorder of addiction."

When an addictive substance is illegal, the addict will have to spend a good deal of time and energy becoming an expert in the predatory world of the black market. If he doesn't, he might not survive. In that case, he will develop characteristics typical of the antisocial personality disorder: lying, cheating, fighting, acting on impulse, and so on. If, on the other hand, the substance is legal and therefore relatively inexpensive and easy to get, then the addict will not have the same pressures. In his case, the repeated episodes of intoxication (and their negative consequences) cause the conflicts with other people, and it will usually take longer for the defense mechanisms associated with addiction to become fully established.

But if all these behavioral changes are a *result* of the addiction, then they aren't really what we mean by "personality" in the first place. A paragraph from the American Psychiatric Association's *Diagnostic and Statistical Manual of Mental Disorders* (*DSM*) is useful here:

> Personality traits are enduring patterns of perceiving, relating to, and thinking about the environment and oneself, and are exhibited in a wide range of important social and personal contexts. It is only when personality traits are inflexible and maladaptive and cause either significant functional impairment or subjective distress that they constitute Personality Disorders. The manifestations of Personality Disorders are often recognized by adolescence or earlier and continue throughout most of adult life, though they often become less obvious in middle or old age.

For the purpose of thinking about the "addictive personality," the key concepts in this definition are "enduring patterns" and "usually recognized by adolescence." The *DSM* contains no diagnostic category called the "addictive personality," because being addicted to a substance doesn't meet these criteria. In other words, although many addicts and alcoholics behave *like* someone with a narcissistic or antisocial personality disorder, unless such a disorder can be shown to have existed *before* the addiction developed, then the current behavior doesn't represent the "enduring pattern" described in the *DSM*.

Again, much of the confusion around the idea of the so-called "addictive personality" is because most of the research on it has been retrospective—that is, conducted on people *after* they became alcoholics and addicts. The question simply cannot be answered by that kind of data. The many studies that have used paper-and-pencil psychological tests provide excellent examples of how misleading research of this kind can be. The Minnesota Multiphasic Personality Inventory (MMPI) is one of the oldest of these tests.

The MMPI is a series of true/false questions (567 in the 1989 revision called the MMPI-2) such as "Do you sleep well at night?" and "Do you sometimes hear voices that other people do not?" It was created originally (in the 1930s) not as a personality test but as a psychiatric illness inventory. The idea was to help busy doctors identify those patients whose medical problems might have more of an emotional or psychological than physical origin. Patients were to be given a questionnaire to fill out in the waiting room. Staff could then score it and present the results to the doctor.

Actually, the MMPI works very well in the sense that it reliably gives the same results with the same subjects year after

year, and so it is a valid way of looking at some kinds of enduring characteristics that might define personality. Whether these
are the best for defining personality is a different question.

In an effort to investigate the question of the "addictive personality," researchers over the years have given the MMPI to
large numbers of alcoholics and addicts. And, of course, the
easiest way to do that is to go to places where there are large
numbers of people whose addiction is definite. Most often that
meant going to hospitals and rehabilitation centers where virtually all of the subjects were in the early stages of recovery
(abstinence, really), and at that point, the MMPI doesn't really
tell us much about the person's personality. It only shows that
newly abstinent alcoholics and addicts act and feel similarly. Is
it so surprising that most of them are irritable, sleeping poorly,
depressed, untrusting, unloved, and unloving?

In dramatic contrast to the similar MMPI results characteristic of early abstinence, the MMPI profiles of recovering alcoholics *with five years of sobriety* fail to demonstrate any consistent
personality type at all. It's a very strong argument that the "addictive personality," as something that is supposed to have preceded the addiction, doesn't exist. Nevertheless, at one point or
another, all kinds of personality characteristics have been postu-
lated as the cause of alcoholism: oral fixation, dependency, depression, anxiety, suppressed homosexuality, impulsivity, and
more. Virtually all of them came from retrospective studies, and
again Vaillant's prospective study provides the antidote.

In *The Natural History of Alcoholism* only one personality
disorder correlated with alcoholism: the antisocial or, as it used

to be known, the sociopathic. But, again, which came first, the alcoholism or the personality disorder? Put simply, the study showed that many sociopaths become alcoholics as a part of their antisocial behavior and that most alcoholics weren't behaving like sociopaths until after they developed alcoholism.

Just to ice the cake of the so-called addictive personality, it's instructive to note that it's perfectly possible to get all sorts of laboratory animals—rats, cats, dogs, and monkeys—addicted to alcohol, cocaine, and heroin. Once addicted, these poor creatures tend to act in quite predictable ways, but it's because they are addicted to a drug, not because they have a particular personality type. And now, researchers have been able to breed strains of mice who are more readily addicted to alcohol. To my mind, that's a pretty strong argument for genetics, not personality.

It is only natural that psychologists and psychiatrists should have hung on to the myth of the addictive personality (as a pre-existing risk factor for developing an addiction)—we tend to be overly fond of our theories—but the fact that many alcoholics and addicts themselves cling to this idea just as tenaciously puzzled me for a long time. At first, I thought it was because the idea of a shared personality type gave them a sense of being alike, of belonging, a kind of "we were different from them all along" group spirit. And perhaps that's true to a certain degree, but it's also true that we humans don't tolerate uncertainty very well: A wrong reason for things being the way they are is better than no reason at all. On the other hand, if the addictive personality is a fiction, at least it's a relatively harmless one.

Having said all this, there are psychological factors that do increase susceptibility to developing addiction, but they are no more "the" cause of the addiction than any other single factor. And, more important, if there are personality traits that predispose people to addiction, they aren't necessarily pathological in and of themselves. Some researchers (notably C. R. Cloninger) have suggested that there are differences in temperament (traits like harm avoidance, novelty seeking, and reward dependence) based in fundamental brain chemistry that may put some people at higher risk for becoming addicted to particular substances. But this whole question is far from settled, and the influence of biological factors in temperamental differences between people may well point back to hereditary factors. In the meantime, there are more important nonpathological psychological factors common to modern behavior in general.

The drive to escape pain, fear, boredom, and all the other negative emotions is simply human, ancient, and rooted in our animal nature. The capacity, however, to quickly and effectively escape such feelings has never been greater than in modern times, and intoxicating drugs aren't the only way of doing it. The list of quick "fixes" for unhappiness reads like a *Who's Who* of the "Anonymous" 12-step groups—gambling, eating, sex as sport, obsessive exercise, TV, Internet gaming, shopping—and is, no doubt, endless.

The problem for modern people is to find a reason for enduring unpleasant or difficult feelings when they can be so easily avoided. And if the escape is socially acceptable (e.g., work) or commercially promoted (e.g., gambling, pornography), then there is hardly anything standing in the way. By the time the negative consequences of these short-term solutions appear, the development of an addiction makes some form of abstinence the only solution.

Again, however, in this chapter I'm concerned primarily with the general idea of susceptibility to addiction, not as much with the specifics. Whether a person becomes addicted to one or more of these means of escape is a question different from that of why he or she sought to escape in the first place. Running from a miserable marriage to the more rewarding arena of the workplace is just like drinking it away at a bar or snorting cocaine at it in a strip club. Any of them may become compulsive, but being a workaholic is considerably more socially acceptable than the other two and therefore not as likely to be regarded as a kind of addiction.

I stress this line of reasoning because people suffering from addictions need to understand that they are not freaks, that much of what passes for normal behavior in this society is only normal in the statistical sense of being average. Much of it is definitely not normal in the sense of being correct or healthy behavior for a human being. Often, it seems, the only difference between a "bad" addiction and a "good" one is the cultural acceptability of the substance or activity involved.

THE SPECTRUM OF ADDICTION

It turns out that the answer to the question posed at the beginning of this chapter—"Why me? Why am I an alcoholic or addict?"—

is pretty straightforward. It's because you are a human being. You are the sort of host in which an addiction can develop.

The answer to the more complicated question "Why am I an alcoholic and Mary is not?" is a little trickier; different people have different combinations of different factors that put them at different levels of risk for developing an addiction to different means of escaping reality. Actually, it's a lot trickier. Sometimes reality is like that. Vaillant says it more specifically in relation to the addiction he was able to study (my paraphrasing):

1. When an intoxicating agent is readily available, especially in rapidly acting forms, the risk of addiction is increased.
2. When a host is demoralized, hasn't learned to use the substance safely, is exposed to heavy use among his peer group, has a genetic loading, or is poorly socialized into the surrounding culture, then the risk of addiction is also increased.

No wonder there is such a high rate of alcoholism among Native Americans; they would appear to have every single risk factor.

I have come to think of the different aspects of susceptibility to addiction as analogous to the primary colors. Just as red, yellow, and blue give all the colors of the spectrum, so too the different combinations of biological, social, and psychological factors create the spectrum of addictions. This idea can be represented by the following diagram:

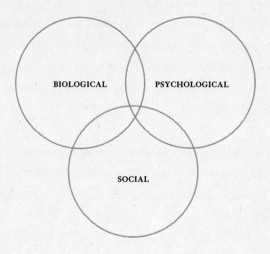

The take-home lesson is consistent with the disease concept of addictions as disorders of automaticity, and it's the same lesson that applies to having any other disease: You may be responsible for having placed yourself at risk for contracting an illness, but you are not responsible for having actually developed it. On the other hand, once you are aware that you have it, you are responsible for doing what you can to recover from it. And that brings us to the question of treatment.

SUMMING UP

1. Simple cause and effect—i.e., "Alcoholism is caused by drinking"—doesn't work. Many people drink, but only some become addicted.

2. In order to understand why only some people become addicted, it is necessary to reiterate the fundamental premise of the disease concept of addiction: An addiction is not behavior, not something someone is *doing*, but something someone *has*, an automatism, a disorder of automaticity.

3. As with all other illnesses, it takes more than an agent of harm (a germ, a toxin, etc.) to develop the disease. There must also be a special vulnerability, a diminished resistance.

4. Biological (both inherited and acquired), psychological, and social factors combine in different ways to make some people more susceptible than others to developing an addiction.

Chapter Three

DOES TREATMENT
"WORK"?

Sometimes I wish I were an orthopedic surgeon. It all seems so straightforward: Take a picture of the problem, correct it, and wait for the body to do its work. Best of all, the patient hardly ever disagrees with you. And if he does, you're not obligated to argue with him about it. This is all a dream, of course, because there are many serious bone and joint problems that cannot be fixed so easily. Still, when I'm frustrated, there are aspects of orthopedics that make it a very attractive medical specialty.

First, making an accurate diagnosis doesn't involve much guesswork; X-rays, MRIs, and CAT scans enable you to see pretty clearly what's wrong. Second, there's a fairly direct relationship between the doctor's abilities and the treatment outcome, so it's possible to learn from your mistakes and improve your skills. Third, many problems have standard treatments, and, as an old medical saying goes, "most people have common diseases." There isn't much controversy over how to deal with anything but the most difficult problems. Last, and best of all, much treatment outcome can be predicted with reasonable certainty. When things don't go as expected, there are usually identifiable reasons, which, in turn, can be recognized and dealt with.

Treating alcoholics and addicts couldn't be more different. First, diagnosis is often unclear. An addiction, unlike a broken bone, cannot be identified at a glance. Unless the patient is going through a definite withdrawal syndrome, the diagnosis of addiction is subjective, a matter of interpreting the patient's experience or behavior over time. Second, since the course of an addiction unfolds over many years, you have to follow patients for a long time to know what effect treatment may have had, which makes it very difficult to improve your skills at providing it. Third, other than those regarding the treatment of withdrawal syndromes, clinicians often have very different and strongly held opinions about what helps people stay sober. As a result, although addiction is a common enough problem, there is no standard treatment. And finally, although to some degree treatment outcome can be predicted for large populations of patients, it's impossible to know how any particular individual will respond.

The result of all this uncertainty is a mass of contradictory opinions and beliefs about who should be treated, what treatment should consist of, and who should provide it. When I was the medical director of a treatment program, all of this confusion put me in an awkward position when trying to respond to the question "What's your success rate?" If it had been a simple matter of not knowing the precise figure, I wouldn't have minded, but that wasn't the problem. The problem was that I *could not* know, nor, despite what they might be saying, could anyone else. The only really honest response I could muster, which very few people wanted to hear, was to ask in return, "What do you mean by *success*?" and "How do you find out if that has been achieved?" and "For how long?"

Over the years, as my irritation with this question grew, I became more and more tempted to respond flippantly, "I'm very successful! The program is full. I'm gainfully employed, and my staff is working together pretty well!" Obviously, that wasn't what people were asking about, and on the surface, I admit, the question seems reasonable. But it harbors a hidden assumption that reflects so much ignorance about what addiction and recovery are all about that it provoked me to anger. The assumption is that there is something *I* (the doctor, nurse, counselor, program) can do *to* the patient that will fix him. It's a fair question for an orthopedic surgeon, as in "Will screwing a metal plate across the fracture fix it?" I suppose that's part of my periodic attraction to orthopedics. Bones generally do what you expect them to. It's also why I put the word *work* in the title of this chapter in quotation marks.

Recovery from addiction is rehabilitation, and, as in all other forms of rehabilitation, treatment doesn't work or not work. The patient works. It seems obvious. If the very nature of addiction is automaticity—the loss of control—then recovery is the restoration of choice, not handing choices over to someone or something else. At the end of this chapter, I'll examine the origins and consequences of the search for a treatment that might "work" on an otherwise passive patient. For now, I simply want to provide an overview of the confusion about treating alcoholics and addicts. In general, it comes from three areas: methods of diagnosis, the nature of treatment, and evaluating treatment outcome.

For as long as medical scientists have been studying addictions, they have used different criteria for diagnosis, different definitions of treatment, and different measures for judging the outcome of those treatments. It's the blind men and the elephant story all over again. In an effort to keep things relatively simple, I'm not going to go into all of these issues in depth—George Vaillant did an excellent job of that in *The Natural History of Alcoholism*—but I do want to convey a sense of why the question of "success rate" is so naive and why it is so difficult to know what the effects of treatment are. In doing so, I hope to drop the question of whether treatment "works" in favor of asking whether or not treatment is helpful and, if so, in what ways.

THE PROBLEM OF DIAGNOSIS

The first source of confusion in evaluating addiction treatment is that for a long time different clinicians and researchers used different criteria for deciding who was and was not an addict. Of course, by the time a patient's addiction becomes severe, diagnosis is easy, but before it reaches that stage, it is not. When the diagnosis isn't clear, researchers have to decide on a set of criteria for selecting subjects, and if the criteria aren't identical, then different studies end up being about different populations. And yet, all of them claim to be about the same problem. To some degree, the resulting confusion has been mitigated by the promulgation of the *DSM* (*The Diagnostic and Statistical Manual of Psychiatry*) criteria; however, that's a relatively recent development, and up to only a few decades ago different studies often used quite different standards for diagnosis.

Also, and contributing another source of confusion, different kinds of drug and alcohol problems have often been studied as if they were stages in the development of a single process, as though drug or alcohol *misuse*, *abuse*, and *dependence* slide seamlessly from one to the other as an addiction progresses. Over the lifetime of any particular addict or alcoholic, that may or may not be true, but it takes years to find out. In fact, it isn't at all unusual for people to have a temporary drug- or alcohol-related problem that *does not* lead to addiction (and therefore isn't affected by treatment).

Over the forty years of Vaillant's study, for example, a substantial number of subjects acquired a few alcohol-related problems (a DUI, an alcohol-related medical problem, marital conflict, or employment problem) but did not go on to become alcoholics. These men could be described as having "misused" alcohol—the sort of people who get into some trouble with drinking at one point in their lives but who never develop the full-blown addiction—this is the college student who "blacks out" once or twice, the woman who gets a single DUI, or the man who "partied" too much over the weekend, missed work on Monday, and was written up for it. If people like this enter treatment and then become subjects in a research study, they will be counted as treatment successes when, in reality, they would have done just as well without any treatment at all.

Some clinicians (and some 12-step group members) believe that anyone who develops any problem with alcohol or drugs inevitably goes on to develop a full-blown addiction, but that's not borne out by good research. Again, *The Natural History of Alcoholism* serves us well here. A large proportion of Vaillant's subjects (60 percent) had at least one alcohol-related problem. An additional 9 percent had two or three. But only about 25 percent of the total sample went on to have more and more problems, eventually meeting diagnostic criteria for either alcohol abuse (four or more alcohol-related problems) or alcoholism itself (four or more alcohol-related problems and physical dependence).

To a certain extent, the inconsistencies in diagnosing drug and alcohol problems are a result of the conceptual error of mistaking behavior for a disease (as discussed in chapter 1). But it's an error reinforced by researchers' need for objective data. Therapists' impressions of patients and patients' descriptions of their own experiences are inherently subjective and very difficult to quantify for statistical analysis. As a result, many researchers have tended to favor behavioral data to make the diagnosis of addiction: how much or how often a subject drinks or uses drugs, for example. It is cheaper and easier to collect this kind of information than it is to interview patients and families in depth, search through police and hospital records, examine employment files, and so on. Perhaps more important, it also lends itself more easily to the short-term research-grant cycles that now predominate in medical science (often only for two to three years at best). Unfortunately, convenience isn't necessarily a dependable path to the truth, and behavioral data alone do not capture the essential experience of addiction: automaticity.

A man who drinks only once a year, for example, but each time he does, loses control and ends up in a self-destructive binge, is an alcoholic by qualitative standards, not quantitative. Similarly, you would never learn from observing her behavior that the woman who no longer uses any cocaine at all is only one hit away from disaster. To be fair, there is some validity in quantifying behavior to make a diagnosis—the man who drinks only occasionally, or not very much when he does, is much less likely to be or to become an alcoholic than one who drinks often or a great deal—but, on the whole, the quantitative approach to diagnosis can never give us the critical part of any patient's story, because it doesn't distinguish between behavior and experience.

In an attempt to avoid this kind of diagnostic confusion, researchers have sought to diagnose addiction by its consequences, by determining the number and duration of the sorts of problems likely to result from frequent intoxication. Although this approach isn't foolproof, it is useful.

In the first place, the development of drug- or alcohol-related problems indicates much better than any quantitative measure of drinking or drug use that something inside has a life of its own. Returning again and again to behavior that ends in trouble suggests that *something* is interfering with learning some fundamental life lessons. But one of the drawbacks of approaching diagnosis this way is that social and cultural factors play a large role in the *kinds* of problems alcoholics and addicts experience.

As a result, unless diagnosis is based on looking for a wide variety of adverse consequences, the data are almost always skewed in some way, and that means that the population studied may not be fully representative of the disorder.

As a simple example, the alcoholics in Vaillant's college sample had far fewer alcohol-related arrests than did their blue-collar counterparts. So, if your criteria for diagnosing alcoholism are heavily weighted toward subjects having social and criminal justice problems (lost jobs, arrests, drunk driving, etc.), your study sample, and hence your conclusions, will be biased. In the same way, using only medical criteria to make the diagnosis (for example, the presence of the alcohol withdrawal syndrome) shifts the population you are studying to those patients whose disease has progressed nearly to the end stage and similarly will prejudice your results. So, the adverse-consequences method of diagnosing addiction can be as misleading as the behavioral.

Once again, *The Natural History of Alcoholism* is very helpful in solving these problems. Vaillant minimized diagnostic errors by requiring at least four or more alcohol-related problems from different areas in the subject's life for the diagnosis of alcohol abuse. This approach gave a much more reliable foundation for diagnosis because it spread the accumulation of alcohol-related problems out over time and into different areas of the subject's life. If, in addition to having four or more alcohol-related problems, the subject also experienced physical withdrawal from alcohol, then he was diagnosed as having alcoholism (alcohol dependence). Over the first forty years of Vaillant's study, out of the original sample of four hundred men, about 25 percent qualified for the diagnosis of alcohol abuse, of which 60 percent were alcohol dependent (about 15 percent of the original four hundred men).

Clearly, Vaillant's method is a better way of distinguishing true alcoholics from people who only have some alcohol-related problems; however, diagnosing an addiction from the number of problems it causes still has some difficulties. It's really an indirect measure of severity—how far the condition has progressed—not of whether or not it exists. And that leaves us in the position of having to wait a long time before we can reliably say it's there. If we were to approach the diagnosis of cancer in the same way, it would mean waiting until a tumor had spread to the lungs, bone, or brain before diagnosing it. Treating it at that late date would bring very different results than if it had been caught and treated early.

The cancer analogy reveals another dilemma in the diagnosis of addictions. When we discover a tumor early, we can get a sense of how aggressive it is by examining its microscopic appearance and determining if it has spread to adjacent tissues and lymph nodes. This is enormously important in choosing the best treatment. But early in the course of an addiction, there is no way of knowing how rapidly it's going to progress, and this adds another complication that makes it difficult to compare different methods of treatment. Treatment that could be effective at one stage of an addiction may not be effective at another.

In the late stages of alcoholism, for example, a patient may have so much brain damage as to be incapable of understanding the need to maintain abstinence. Or he may have fallen into such despair that he no longer believes he has anything to live for. And at the other end of the scale, until an addict has suffered some really serious consequences of his addiction (AA's "hitting bottom"), he may still believe he can control his use. In both cases, treatment isn't likely to be very helpful, and it's important to know that when trying to understand what sort of treatment helps whom.

For all these reasons, then, it is important that diagnosis flow from an understanding of what the condition *is*, not simply from tabulating what people do or the number of problems they acquire as a result of doing it. With that in mind, I'd like to restate the main thesis of this book: Addictions are automatisms that can be arrested but not eliminated. Someday there may well be an objective way of visualizing the neurophysiological underpinnings of such an automatism, and then the diagnosis will be as clear to us as a fractured femur is to an orthopedist. But for now, the best way to an accurate diagnosis is still a careful clinical interview aimed at finding out whether the patient is struggling to control something that has developed a life of its own.

WHAT IS TREATMENT?

In addition to having had different criteria for diagnosis, clinicians and researchers have also had different standards for what they mean by *treatment*. Do mandatory classes after a DUI arrest qualify as treatment? Marital counseling for the addict and spouse? Does going through detox alone mean that an addict has been treated? How about taking a medication that is supposed to reduce craving? Over the years, all these and more have been called treatment and, to the casual reader, pass for the same thing, adding yet more confusion as to whether or not treatment "works."

In the absence of any consensus on what it means to treat an addiction, all manner of simplistic medical or psychological procedures (hypnosis, medication, aversive conditioning, acupuncture, etc.) persist without good evidence of any long-term benefit. It's natural enough for alcoholics and addicts themselves to want to be "fixed" by something that "works." Having someone else do something for you is more of the passive dependence that marks the addiction itself. But these sorts of treatments are attractive to other people as well and not only to drug companies eager to profit from selling a "cure."

Passive forms of treatment are attractive to medical scientists because they bypass two confounding variables that make studying the effects of treatment difficult: first, individual variations among patients (severity of addiction, level of motivation, mental capacity, physical health, and so on); and, second, all the variables connected with the skill and experience of the person providing the treatment.

It doesn't really matter, for example, why you're taking disulfiram (Antabuse) or who prescribes it; you'll get sick if you drink while taking it in any case. In the same way, the technician who gives you a martini followed by a drug that makes you vomit (the Schick method of aversive conditioning) doesn't have to know much about how the treatment is supposed to work. Either the negative association between drinking and getting sick will stick or it won't. In both cases, it's easy for medical researchers to ask whether Antabuse or aversive conditioning "works." The patient isn't being asked to do anything, and there is no personal influence from the individual providing the treatment.

In reality, no treatment program relies solely on these simplistic treatment methods. Virtually all of them include counseling, family therapy, and education of one kind or another, and all these forms of treatment are highly dependent on the personal qualities of the individual offering it. Several decades ago, the psychiatrist Jerome Frank discovered this principle in researching why so many different kinds of psychotherapy seemed to work equally well. Adherents of the various schools of psychotherapy certainly believed that their differences were important, yet none seemed more successful than any other.

Frank concluded first that the central problem bringing people to psychotherapy was demoralization and, second, that the different kinds of psychotherapy shared several factors that, if successful, encouraged patients to face their difficulties anew. Subsequent studies have confirmed that among the most important of these factors are the therapist's personal characteristics—qualitites such as warmth, genuineness, capacity for nonjudgmental regard, and so on. For the purposes of this book, there is no need to delve further into this otherwise very interesting topic. The point is that many of the factors that make psychotherapy successful are extremely difficult to standardize and measure quantitatively. And that, in turn, makes this kind of treatment difficult to study. It also makes simplistic treatments all the more attractive to people who are searching for something that "works."

The bottom line is that there is no standard psychotherapeutic treatment for addiction, although virtually everything under the sun has been tried: hypnotic suggestion, cognitive behavioral therapy, psychoanalysis, rational emotive behavior therapy, behavioral conditioning, primal scream, you name it. None of them has been shown to be any more or less "successful" in treating alcoholism or drug addiction.

THE PROBLEM OF MEASURING
TREATMENT OUTCOME

Since those of us who work with addicts and alcoholics haven't been able to agree on what these disorders are or on how to treat them, it shouldn't come as a surprise that we also haven't been able to agree on the goal of treatment. As a result, different studies have adopted very different criteria for what is meant by a successful treatment outcome. Is it total abstinence? Or is it just a reduction in the amount or frequency of drinking or drug use? Or something else?

Many clinicians, for example, feel that the goal of total abstinence is unreasonable, a throwback to the moralistic or Puritanical view, which cast alcoholics and addicts as sinners. It sounds like a very modern and enlightened perspective, but if abstinence isn't the goal of treatment, then what is? "Mostly" abstinent? If so, then what exactly does that mean? Is one "slip," say, a few days of drinking within several months of abstinence, still a success? What if the patient loses his job or is arrested for a DUI during that one slip? Does that mean treatment failed? What if the patient hadn't been arrested or his supervisor had looked the other way? Would treatment then have been a success? Is this a valid foundation for judging the effect of treatment? And this is just the beginning of the problems of measuring treatment outcome. So far I've only brought up the difficulties of defining treatment goals; there are other issues that are just as serious. One of the most important is how long patients are followed after they have completed treatment.

As an example, in the 1970s a group of behavioral scientists abandoned abstinence as the goal of treatment and sought to train alcoholics to control their drinking. Twenty alcoholics from a VA hospital took part in an intense program of behavioral modification aimed at teaching them to moderate their drinking. At a six months' follow-up, the outcome data looked very good: The majority of the patients reported that they were drinking substantially less than they had before treatment. Aside from the fact that the data were self-reported and therefore somewhat suspect (patients were contacted by phone and asked how they were doing), six months is simply not long enough to tell us anything definitive about the effects of any treatment. Many alcoholics, without any treatment at all, have had periods of reduced or nonproblematic drinking for periods of six months. The test of time for recovery from addiction is measured in years, not months.

In fact, when a different group of researchers followed up on the same patients ten years later, a completely different picture emerged. Only one of the original twenty subjects was judged to have continued to drink without problems, and it was doubtful that this man had been truly alcoholic in the first place. Four of the others had died of alcohol-related causes, and eight had continued to drink with damaging consequences. Those who were doing well hadn't learned to control their drinking; they had become abstinent.

There are still more sources of outcome confusion. The book *Drug Abuse Treatment: A National Study of Effectiveness* (funded by the federal government and gleefully subtitled "Treatment Works!") provides an instructive example and brings to mind Disraeli's remark: "There are three kinds of lies: lies, damned lies, and statistics."

This study followed up on several thousand drug addicts one year after they had been in either a residential treatment setting, an out-patient clinic, or a methadone maintenance program. The results seemed far better than any program I was familiar with and were very puzzling. A careful examination of the footnotes to the outcome tables and graphs revealed the source of my confusion: About half of the patients who began treatment weren't included in the final calculations of outcome. Why? Because they had dropped out within the first twelve weeks of the study. In other words, the inability to keep a patient in treatment beyond the first twelve weeks wasn't counted as a treatment failure! I suppose there is some justification for such reasoning, but it seems dubious. It has been noted, for example, that the 12-step programs also suffer from the same problem: Many addicts and alcoholics, especially early in the course of their addiction, quit going to meetings before twelve weeks have passed. But AA and its cousins aren't professionally run programs. They don't claim to be able to act upon a patient who wants to remain passive while someone else does something for him.

There are many other, if less dramatic, examples of studies based on inadequate outcome data. The end result is a terrible muddle about whether or not treatment even helps, let alone which kind of treatment is best. On the other hand, studies that have followed reliably diagnosed alcoholics for long enough periods of time reveal what clinicians and AAs have known for a long time: Abstinence is necessary for recovery. The third group of subjects in *The Natural History of Alcoholism* demonstrates it clearly.

This third group consisted of one hundred men and women who entered the study after going through a detox program in the Boston area. They were then followed prospectively for the next eight years. The fact that the researchers were able to maintain contact with nearly all these patients is astonishing in and of itself. Alcoholics are notoriously difficult to track over such a long period of time: They lose their jobs, move away from friends and families, get sick and are hospitalized (and sometimes die), get arrested and go to jail, and so on, all of which makes them very hard to trace. Nevertheless, in this study, all but six of the original one hundred subjects were followed for the whole eight years. The results were dramatic and can be put fairly simply: Over the eight years after detox, both the number of patients who became abstinent *and* the number of patients who died steadily increased. On the other hand, the number of patients who kept on drinking decreased and, for the most part, were the ones dying.

Vaillant's study teaches the same lesson that the long-term follow-up of the controlled-drinking experiments taught: If you follow true alcoholics for *years*, you discover that those who continue to drink get worse and those who remain abstinent don't. Presumably, the same is true for all other addictions.

As a side note, five of Vaillant's original one hundred clinic patients went back to nonproblematic drinking after treatment. They are the exceptions that prove the rule. Vaillant described these five patients as "very different from the other 95. At first admission, they had enjoyed far greater social stability; they had experienced far shorter periods of active alcoholic drinking; and three of them had never required previous detox." In other words, they were people who had had enough problems with drinking to land in treatment but who were never physically addicted and therefore didn't have to become abstinent in order to stop the progression of the disease.

The purpose of going into all the problems associated with diagnosis, treatment, and treatment outcome is twofold: first, to show why it is so difficult to make sense of all the different studies and claims of success in treating alcoholics and addicts, and, second, to set the stage for understanding recovery from a different perspective. To do that, we first need to understand that addictions are automatisms—conditions that cannot be cured but that can be made dormant through abstinence. Second, we need to take the focus off what we, the treatment professionals, do *to* addicts and alcoholics and ask what they do *for themselves* to maintain abstinence.

One note to conclude this section. AA and the other 12-step programs should not be judged in the same way that we evaluate professionally run treatment programs. *Treatment* generally means something administered or conducted by a professional. The 12-step programs, by contrast, are overtly and intentionally *not* run by professionals but by recovering addicts and alcoholics themselves. The distinction is important because a recovering addict cannot "receive" the 12 steps in the same sense that he can receive treatment from a professional. In AA, the alcoholic is working among equals—fellow addicts and alcoholics—not placing himself under the care of someone who is getting paid to do something for him. Professional treatment and 12-step participation aren't incompatible; they just aren't the same kind of thing and shouldn't be compared as though they were.

RECOVERY FROM ADDICTION

ABSTINENCE—NECESSARY BUT INSUFFICIENT

Recovery from addiction means more than quitting. It means, as AAs say, "staying quit." It means not beginning again. Once the difference between quitting and not starting again became clear to me, I began to interview patients in a new way. Rather than dwelling on why they had continued doing what was so obviously bad for them, I began to ask them if they had had any periods of abstinence and, if so, what they had been doing at the time.

What I discovered surprised me. If they hadn't been abstinent simply by "white-knuckling it," they had almost always been active in one of the 12-step groups (periods of enforced abstinence as a result of being in hospital or jail didn't count). I also learned that when they'd started using or drinking again, it was almost always *after* they'd stopped going to meetings, stopped talking with their sponsor, stopped working on the steps, or in some other way stopped actively participating in a good 12-step program.

After many years of listening to these stories, I began to hear them as variations on the same two themes: forgetting and not caring. If a patient had achieved a significant period of abstinence (on the order of months), he had begun drinking or using drugs again in one of two ways: Either he forgot that, for him, there was no such thing as "just one" (drink, hit, snort, whatever), or else he knew it and had gotten into such a state of emotional distress that he didn't care.

Forgetting and not caring don't operate entirely separately, but for the purposes of thinking simply about how people begin again (and what they can do to avoid it), it's useful to note that they are different. The important point is that if a patient had become abstinent and then relapsed, it was almost always true either that he had never become active in a 12-step group or that he had been active and stopped going.

A typical story of relapse by forgetting would go something like this:

"So, you say you were sober for how long last year?" I ask.

"Oh, about six months, I guess."

"What were you doing then . . . I mean, were you going to AA or anything?"

"Yeah, I was doing great there for a while, Doc. I was going to three meetings a week, and I was starting to work on my fourth step with my sponsor. At first my wife was real happy, but then it began to bug her that I was out at night so much. She even thought I was getting too friendly with some of the gals at the meetings."

"Was she going to her Al-Anon meetings?"

"Yeah, she was going for a while, but then she said the meetings were making her depressed, so she stopped going."

"What happened then?"

"Well, let's see . . . Oh yeah, my sponsor had to move because of his job, so we kind of lost touch. Anyway, he was getting on my back 'cause I wasn't going to all the meetings he wanted me to. So, I just quit calling him."

"So how did you get started drinking again? I mean where were you when you had the first one? What were you thinking?"

"Let's see. . . . Oh yeah, I remember. Yeah, it was about six months after I went through the program. I was at a ball game with my buddy Mike. He was having a beer and offered me one. At first I said no, but then I thought, 'Hell, one beer won't hurt me.'"

"And when was that?"

"About a month ago. I don't know why I can't control it, Doc. I must have something real wrong inside. Maybe I'm just self-destructive. What do you think?"

"Were you thinking about 'destroying yourself' at the
ball game when you had that beer?"

"Hell no! Are you crazy? I was having a good time,
and I just had a couple that night. It really didn't
get out of hand until the next weekend. That's
when my wife and I had a big fight. I guess I
forgot what I learned in the program."

This kind of forgetting isn't limited to people with addictions. If you think of going to meetings as "taking your medicine," then what this man told me is entirely consistent with what we find in medical practice generally: Only 26 percent of patients take their medications exactly as prescribed. We've all done it. You go to your doctor with a fever and terrible sore throat. She prescribes a course of penicillin lasting a week, suggests you take some aspirin, and tells you to rest for a while. A few days later your throat begins to feel better, and you jump back into your life. And then you forget to take the penicillin as it was prescribed. Two days later the infection comes back.

*Lesson: It's hard to remember that something
is wrong when nothing hurts.*

Translated to the problem of recovering from addiction, the same lesson goes like this: It's hard for people to remember how much they need their 12-step program when, as a result of having become sober, things start to get better. Relapse by forgetting is common only in the course of an addiction, before people are really convinced that their struggle for control is doomed to failure. More rarely, people forget after years of abstinence. In those cases, the culprit is complacency: People quit going to meetings and gradually forget what they had learned so many years before.

People who relapse as a result of not caring are in a different position. They may know very well that "there is no such thing as one" but are so beside themselves with grief, fear, shame, rage, or boredom that they simply can't stand it. If they think about it at all, their thoughts go something like this: "If this is how it feels to be sober, the hell with it. I was just as miserable when I was drinking; at least then I had a little relief."

A number of my patients who relapsed in this way were as perplexed as I was about how it had happened. They had been going to their 12-step meetings and had started drinking or using again anyway. How could that be? Eventually, as I learned to ask for specifics—the types of meetings they had been going to, whether they had been sharing at the meetings, if they had gotten a sponsor, what they had learned from the steps, if they had been of service, and so on—I nearly always found that they had not been participating wholeheartedly. *Why* they had been holding back then became the focus of the assessment and to a large degree shaped the treatment plan.

The particular emotional "trigger" for starting up again can take many different forms—getting fired, having a fight with a spouse, becoming physically ill or depressed—all sorts of adverse events which the person simply can't cope with. But no trigger works without a spring. And in the case of the addict or alcoholic who isn't working a good 12-step program, that spring is being wound up tighter and tighter as time passes. Eventually, the slightest disturbance can set it off. AAs call it being a "dry drunk": behaving in all the destructive ways addicts and alcoholics typically behave but without actually drinking or using or, in other words, abstinent but not happy about it.

Treatment strategies aimed at helping people "stay quit" are lumped together in the category of "relapse prevention." I suppose that's acceptable as long as *relapse* isn't being used to describe something inherent in the addiction itself, as in the expression "Addictions are chronic relapsing illnesses." Used in this way, the word *relapse* can imply that the patient is a helpless victim of the disease, as in the phrase "He *had* a relapse." Wrong. The only thing the patient *has* is the addiction itself. If he started again, it was something he *did*, not something that happened to him. Yes, after he began using or drinking again, something that has a life of its own took over, but that was *after* he chose to drink or use.

When an addiction is described as a "chronic and relapsing brain disease," it can suggest to patients that no matter what they do, a relapse can still hit, as it were, "out of the blue." It supports the avoidance of responsibility and ultimately breeds a kind of self-serving fatalism. Not long ago, a man I was evaluating for a diversion program tried to twist the meaning of the word *relapse* in just this way, hoping to be excused for having chosen to use again. A cocaine-addicted physician, he said to me, "Come on. You're a doctor, you know this is a chronic relapsing disease." No, it is not. Addictions don't relapse; people relapse. Addicts and alcoholics must know from the outset of treatment that relapse is not inevitable, that it is possible and necessary to make choices and take actions that maintain sobriety. Isn't that obvious? If people couldn't choose not to drink or use again, how could anyone recover?

Of course, in simplifying the process of relapse down to forgetting and not caring, I haven't done justice to the complexities involved. Where mere ignorance ends and motivated forgetting begins is rarely clear, and the suffering that leads to relapse can range from trivial to profound, but the overall picture remains the same. More important, it provides a way of thinking about what the goal of treatment ought to be.

BEYOND ABSTINENCE:
THE GOAL OF TREATMENT

Again, let's start from this simple fact: Tens of thousands of alcoholics and addicts have recovered through their work in 12-step programs. It's also true that many alcoholics and addicts, for a whole variety of reasons, don't want to become members of such a group. Perhaps they're turned off by the spiritual element of the program. Maybe they think AA is a cult. Others believe they can stay sober without any help from anyone else. Still others turn to sanctioned forms of drug dependence (methadone or buprenorphine maintenance). All these exceptions notwithstanding, it is an indisputable fact that an enormous number of people attribute their recovery to their work on the 12 steps.

To me, recognition and acceptance of this fact is analogous to Dr. Edward Jenner's discovery of vaccination as the way to prevent smallpox. In the late 1700s, smallpox was endemic throughout England. Many people died of it or bore the hideous facial scars it left behind. At the same time, it was common knowledge among countryfolk that milkmaids never got the disease; hence the songs about milkmaids' beautiful complexions. Jenner believed that these women were protected from smallpox because they had already had the similar but much milder disease cowpox. He then applied his insight by intentionally infecting people who hadn't yet had smallpox with cowpox. Our very word for this procedure, *vaccination*, comes from the Latin root for "cow," *vacca*, and many of our fundamental concepts of immunity begin with Jenner's work.

The point is that Jenner didn't invent the solution to smallpox out of thin air. The solution already existed. What was left to medical science was to understand it and then to adopt and spread its use. I believe the same is true for recovery from alcohol and drug addiction. If we understand addictions as automatisms, if we understand that recovery is based on abstinence, if we understand that people relapse because they forget or stop caring, and, finally, if we understand how working a 12-step program helps people remember and care, then the goal of treatment must go beyond mere abstinence. Abstinence is necessary because it is the foundation for becoming a dedicated active member of a 12-step group.

For some professionals, the idea that the alcoholic has to be abstinent to begin recovery seems paradoxical. After all, if the patient had been able to stay sober, he wouldn't be coming to treatment. What sort of treatment starts by asking the patient to do the very thing he needs treatment to help him to do? The psychologist G. Alan Marlatt, who has made a detailed study of relapse behavior, puts it this way: "First we tell the patient he is powerless, then we tell him to exert control—to abstain!" Although Dr. Marlatt has misunderstood what alcoholics mean by *powerlessness*—that something inside has developed a life of its own—the paradox he poses has to be addressed.

If abstinence alone were the goal of treatment, then it would indeed be absurd to require it for treatment to proceed. But mere abstinence isn't the goal. The goal is recovery—the restoration of a fully human life with all its trials and tribulations—and recovery can't be attained without abstinence. Treatment doesn't start by asking the patient to do something he can't do; it starts with something he can do: go to 12-step meetings, then look for a sponsor, then begin to work the steps, and so on. He won't do any of that if he's still drinking or using. Abstinence isn't the end of treatment; it's the beginning of recovery.

This principle is at the heart of the 12-step programs: The only "qualification" for membership is a desire not to drink or use. People who are intoxicated may not be invited to speak at meetings, but unless they make trouble, they are welcome to be there. So, if my simplification of how addicts and alcoholics begin again is right—if people relapse as a result of forgetting and/or not caring—then the remaining question is this: How does participating in a 12-step program help people remember and care?

First, going to meetings helps you remember that you have an addiction. Each time you hear someone share his or her experience at a meeting, you realize, "Oh yes, that's me. That's what happened to me." You remember that having an addiction means that there is no such thing as one drink, hit, joint, snort, toke, pipe, whatever. It means that the automatism is never going to go away but that it can be kept dormant. In time, going to meetings means more than merely listening to others. It means speaking at the meetings yourself, making a commitment to set up the chairs, make the coffee, distribute the literature, and so on—small acts of service that put you at the right place, at the right time, with the right kind of attitude to be reminded that you have an addiction. Going to meetings regularly is the cost of remembering.

I cannot count the number of times I've had this sort of conversation with patients who are having trouble staying sober because they don't understand the principle of paying for the gift of remembering with their own efforts:

> "Have you gone to AA meetings?" I ask.
>
> "Yeah, I went to some. They didn't do anything
>   for me."
>
> "That may be, but did you participate? Did you
>   share? Did you read the book?"
>
> "Well, I guess I really didn't . . ."
>
> "Tell me something. If you went to college but didn't
>   listen to the lectures, didn't read the books, and
>   didn't hand in your assignments, would you say,
>   'It didn't work for me'?"
>
> "No. I guess not, Doc. You've got a point."

Early on in these sorts of discussions, many patients ask, "How long do I have to go to these meetings?" My AA mentor,

Tom Redgate, once gave this wonderful reply to a skeptical patient: "You have to keep going until you want to." Perhaps that's a little too cryptic (Tom was a master of aphorisms), so I'll try to explain. If you go to meetings regularly, especially when you don't particularly want to, you might discover why you ought to. You might learn that nothing of any lasting value comes without effort. When you've learned that lesson, then you will probably want to take advantage of anything and everything that helps you make those efforts. Again, AA has some neat aphorisms for this idea: "Fake it till you make it" and, as noted previously, "Bring your body; your mind will follow." Left to its own devices, the mind forgets.

Second, as a result of actually working on the 12 steps—reading the literature, writing about your own experiences, talking with a sponsor, taking the suggested actions—you become more capable of accepting that suffering is an inevitable part of life, and that, in turn, will help you avoid the state of not caring about what will happen if you begin to drink or use again. Since the connection between suffering and spiritual awakening is the main point of the next chapter, I'll let that statement stand without further elaboration for now.

In summary, then, and stated as simply as possible, I believe that the guiding principle for treating alcoholics and addicts is this:

> *The goal of treatment is to help patients*
> *overcome obstacles to becoming dedicated,*
> *active members of a 12-step group.*

Imagine you've come to see me for treatment of your addiction. We say hello, I offer you a seat, and then I begin to listen to your story. But I'm not listening without a framework, a context. I know that tens of thousands of people have recovered from alcoholism and drug addiction by becoming active members of one of the 12-step groups. Since, at this point, I have no reason to believe that you're fundamentally different from all those people, I naturally wonder why you haven't been able to do what they have. What's prevented you from becoming a dedicated, active member of a 12-step group? Perhaps you haven't yet really understood what addiction is. Perhaps you don't really believe that you'll never be able to "control" it. Maybe you are so anxious or depressed that you haven't been able to make yourself go to meetings. Maybe you're turned off by the emphasis on a Higher Power. Maybe you're afraid AA will rob you of your individuality. Maybe you're just angry with all the people telling you what you should do. There can be many different and serious obstacles, but the principle that treatment consists of helping people overcome them remains the same.

I'm sure that many of the counselors and nurses I supervised over the years often thought of me as a broken record. Right in the middle of their talking about a patient's difficult relationship with his wife, for example, I would interrupt and ask, "But how is that an obstacle to his becoming a dedicated member of AA? He isn't really coming to see us for the marriage. There may be some serious problems there, but he came to us because he hasn't been able to stay sober. He's quit in the past, yes, but then he's started again. Did he forget what would happen if he had 'just one'? Or did he know what would happen and not care? Does the marital problem have something to do with that?" Sometimes it did, and then it became a legitimate concern of treatment. But if it didn't, and we focused on it during treatment, then we ran the risk of diverting the patient from the most important part of recovery: becoming a dedicated, active member of a 12-step group.

In trying to understand what a particular patient's obstacles—and motivations—may be, I have found it very useful to ask the following questions:

1. Why is the patient coming to treatment now? Why not yesterday, last week, last month? What changed? And why has it resulted in his coming to treatment?

2. Has the patient ever been abstinent? If so, for how long? What was he doing during that period?

3. Has the patient ever been in treatment before? If so, what happened after treatment?

4. Has the patient ever been active in 12-step? If not, why not?

5. If the patient was active in 12-step, for how long and how involved was he? Did he have a sponsor? Did he work the steps? Did he take commitments at meetings? Did he become active in service work? If not, why not?

6. If the patient was active in 12-step and then began drinking or using again, did his participation stop or change? Why?

There can be a bewildering variety of answers to these questions. In general, however, they break down into four areas: biological, emotional, cognitive, and spiritual. I think of them as the dimensions of treatment.

THE DIMENSIONS OF
TREATMENT: BIOLOGICAL

Obviously, no one can begin the work of not starting again until they have first quit. Thus, the first obstacle to recovery that many alcoholics and addicts have to face is a nasty withdrawal syndrome.

These days almost everyone knows that the careful use of medication can make it easier to withdraw from an addictive drug. I say "careful" not just in the sense of watching the dosage and duration of such treatment but also in terms of deciding whether or not the use of medication is even really necessary. In our zeal to help people, it's very easy for physicians to make things worse by transferring a patient's addiction from one drug to another—for example, from alcohol to a benzodiazepine (e g., Valium). Without intending to, I've done it myself. At the same time, the judicious use of drugs to treat the various withdrawal syndromes may be lifesaving.

In the following sections, I'd like to give a brief overview of "detoxification" from each of the major types of drugs people become addicted to: the CNS (central nervous system) depressants, the CNS stimulants, the opiates, and the hallucinogens.

Readers who have no particular interest in this initial phase of treatment or in the psychopharmacology of addictive drugs may wish to skip this section. It isn't essential for understanding the long-term goal of treatment.

CNS (Central Nervous System) Depressants

Drugs in this category are known to physicians as "sedatives," "hypnotics," and "minor tranquilizers." On the street they're called "downers." The oldest member of this group is alcohol, followed by all of the barbiturates (Seconal, Nembutal, Amytal, etc.), a host of once-popular but now mostly discontinued drugs (Miltown, Quaalude, Placidyl, Doriden), and last, the widely prescribed benzodiazepines (Librium, Valium, Klonopin, and their relatives).

All of these substances depress or decrease the activity of the cells in the central nervous system (the brain and the spinal cord). Gradually, the system adapts by pushing back, as it were, to a normal level of activity. Users experience this effect as "tolerance." Then, in order to recapture the original effect of the drug (resulting from decreased brain activity), they have to increase the dose of the drug. People who have become tolerant to these drugs can wind up taking doses that would be lethal to anyone who was not adapted to them, and yet the person who has developed tolerance functions normally. It's only when the addict tries to stop or cut down his use that problems, in the form of the withdrawal syndrome, develop. How severe that syndrome will be depends on how much of the drug he's been taking, for how long, how abruptly he stops, and the nature of the drug itself.

Imagine the brain as a big coil spring. Drinking a fifth of vodka a day is like putting a heavy weight on the spring. If that weight is removed suddenly, the spring shoots up to a level beyond its normal height. Exactly how high depends upon how hard it was pushed down and how suddenly it's released. In this analogy, "springing up" means increased brain activity.

If, when the alcohol (or other CNS depressant) is stopped, brain activity springs up only a little, then the patient becomes nervous, is easily startled, and doesn't sleep well. If it springs up a little higher, the brain begins to signal the muscles to move without the patient intending it—the result being "tremors" or "shakes." Next, the brain may become so active as to produce sights and sounds when nothing is there—hallucinations. (The traditional medical term for the combination of hallucinations and tremors in alcohol withdrawal is *delirium tremens*, or D.T.'s). Finally, if the brain becomes so active that the patient cannot sleep for several days, it may produce epileptic-like seizures, which, in turn, can result in severe injury. For these reasons, if there's a chance that someone might experience a severe CNS-depressant withdrawal, he should be evaluated by an experienced medical professional *before* he decides to stop on his own.

Treatment of CNS-depressant withdrawal is easiest and safest when the patient comes in to the hospital still taking the drugs or drinking. The principle of managing the withdrawal safely is to prevent the spring from being released abruptly. We do that by giving the patient a drug of the same type but one that takes the body longer to get rid of, thereby slowing down the rate at which the spring pops back to normal. For example, it takes the body only about four to six hours to remove alcohol from the blood. That's pretty fast and therefore dangerous. But it takes the body about 24 to 48 hours to remove another CNS depressant, diazepam (Valium). As a result, I substitute the longer-acting diazepam for the shorter-acting alcohol, so that the patient's brain cells return to their normal level of activity more slowly, which makes withdrawal safer. In practice, dosage and duration of treatment has to be tailored to the individual patient, and ideally this is done by well-trained professionals. Finding the right balance between too much and too little medication is a matter of good clinical judgment, which, in turn, comes from experience. Addiction to the longer-acting CNS depressants (e.g., Doriden) often requires very lengthy treatment with an even longer-acting sedative, usually phenobarbital.

Although I've never seen it referred to in medical books, there does seem to be a "momentum" component in CNS-depressant withdrawal. It's much easier (and therefore safer) to treat the withdrawal syndrome by getting control of it early rather than waiting for symptoms to show up and then giving medication "as needed." It's like having to get a large boulder down from the top of a steep hill: It's much easier to control it from the very beginning than to wait until it gets going and then try to control it.

CNS STIMULANTS

Widely abused drugs in this category include the amphetamines (dextroamphetamine, methamphetamine), cocaine (including freebase and "crack"), and some other stimulants (methylphenidate). These chemicals appear to act first by forcing the release and then slowing the removal of naturally occurring CNS neurotransmitters that stimulate brain cells and nerves, possibly dopamine and noradrenaline. Doctors were slow to recognize that patients experience a withdrawal syndrome when they stopped taking speed or coke, because we were used to associating withdrawal with tangible *physical* symptoms, not the less obvious *psychological* symptoms that predominate in this kind of withdrawal. Psychological symptoms—exhaustion, depression, agitation—however, are no less a reflection of altered brain chemistry than the more obvious physical symptoms of withdrawal from a CNS depressant.

By the time people are getting into serious trouble with cocaine (at the time of this writing, probably the most widely used drug in this group), they are often using it in a pattern of binges or "runs." These binges usually last two or three days and often end in physical and psychological exhaustion, along with a resurgence of all the autonomic functions (notably eating and sleeping) that were suppressed by the stimulant drug. Typically, after "crashing," these patients do little other than sleep and eat for several days before they become "normal" again. Occasionally, they develop a paranoid psychosis and need to be hospitalized.

If the patient is not psychotic, it's rarely necessary to use medications to help a stimulant addict through withdrawal. By the time the patient gets to a residential treatment program, it's usually enough to point him toward the bed and say "Good night." Sometimes, a little Valium can help an agitated patient get to sleep, but once out, the patient doesn't need too much help. We provide a safe environment, nutritious food in large amounts (patients don't eat much during stimulant binges), and medical attention for whatever other medical problems may have resulted from the cocaine use. Sleeping pills and tranquilizers may be helpful temporarily, but they aren't really critical. Patients coming to an outpatient treatment setting, particularly if they're in the middle of a binge, might well benefit from medication to reduce craving, but as yet, no such medication has been proven to be particularly effective.

The craving for cocaine doesn't usually reappear for several days after the binge is over. Again, I haven't found it necessary to treat this stage of withdrawal with drugs (all of which are still experimental at the time of this writing), but, then, most of my patients have been in a hospital or residential setting while these urges die down. Many of them have said that if they hadn't been contained in a "safe haven" they wouldn't have been able to resist the craving to use again.

Opioids

The opioids (natural and man-made) are the only class of drugs properly called narcotics. This group includes mild and moderate pain relievers like codeine, hydrocodone (Vicodin), oxycodone (Percodan, Oxycontin), propoxyphene (Darvon), and various prescription cough suppressants and antidiarrheals. It also includes the more potent pain medications morphine, meperidine (Demerol), and the infamous heroin, but, as a class, their use is age-old. Ancient Greek physicians were well aware of the narcotic power in the sap of the opium poppy bulb and called the state it produced *ataraxia,* or "peace of mind." No wonder these drugs are so potently addicting. The history of opiate use, abuse, and dependence in America is an extraordinary and little known story. Anyone at all interested will find fascinating reading in *Licit and Illicit Drugs* by Edward M. Brecher, *The American Disease* by David F. Musto, and *Addicts Who Survived* by David Courtwright, Herman Joseph, and Don Des Jarlais.

What is peculiar about the withdrawal from opiates is that while it doesn't look so terrible from the outside, from the inside it is apparently agonizing. An alcoholic who is so tremulous that he can hardly hold a glass of water will often respond that he's OK when asked how he's feeling. By contrast, a heroin addict on the third day of withdrawal won't look too bad—a runny nose, some diarrhea, and goose bumps—but, when asked how he feels, will tell you he's dying. And the moment you turn around, he's just as likely to have left the program to "take care of business" (meaning "use").

Withdrawal from opiates triggers one of the most powerful hungers known to human beings. My experience in treating opiate addicts, like that of many of my colleagues, hasn't been very successful over the long haul. Reluctantly, I advise some, who repeatedly fail to maintain long-term abstinence, to enter a methadone maintenance program. I say reluctantly, because methadone is just as hard to quit as heroin, but it does have the virtue of being legal and long-acting enough as to require only one dose a day. Once they are no longer under the compulsion to quell their drug craving, patients have a chance to establish some stability in their lives. After that, if they wish, they can attempt the long and gradual withdrawal from methadone. Some patients have now had good results in handling the withdrawal from oxycodone, hydrocodone, and codeine with the new drug buprenorphine (Buprenex, Subutex, and Suboxone), but the problem of later withdrawing from these drugs remains. These treatments are really substitute addictions, not a "cure."

HALLUCINOGENS

This group of drugs includes all the "alphabet" drugs—LSD, MDA, MDMA (Ecstasy), STP—as well as various plant products from mushrooms (psilocybin), cacti (mescaline, peyote), and the ubiquitous marijuana (cannabis). Although some physicians have identified a physical withdrawal from these drugs, if it exists it doesn't seem severe. I'll keep an open mind, but most of the patients I've treated didn't go back to hallucinogen use to satisfy a drug hunger but simply because they had no particular motivation to remain abstinent. Hallucinogen use (particularly that of marijuana) had become a way of life. There weren't any dramatic adverse consequences to using it, and people didn't go back to it so much from any sort of "craving" as from the absence of anything better in their lives.

In addition to needing treatment for withdrawal, patients may very well have other physical problems that need to be treated in order for rehabilitation to proceed. I'm not going to list them here. Suffice it to say that a balanced approach to treatment will include a good physical exam by a qualified health-care professional followed by whatever treatment may be necessary.

THE DIMENSIONS OF TREATMENT: EMOTIONAL

Practicing (meaning "currently drinking and/or using") alcoholics and addicts are among the most obnoxious, violent, manipulative, dishonest, and pathetic patients I have ever dealt with. In my years as an emergency room doctor, I confess I dreaded nothing quite so much as a call from the nurse: "Doctor, the cops have an injured drunk in Room 1," or "There's a heroin overdose in Room 2; I'll get the restraints." Only years later, after I'd had the experience of working with the same patients in the process of recovery, did I begin to feel any compassion for them. Physicians and nurses have a particular dislike for patients who blatantly bring harm upon themselves and then demand help. Reflexively, we think of the thirty-six-year-old mother of two in the next room, dying of metastatic breast cancer, who would have gone through anything to live, but for whom nothing could be done. It just doesn't seem right.

To be addicted is to be in the grips of an automatism, a psychobiological mechanism. As it grows, it demands more and more time and energy, and the addict is forced to compromise or sacrifice everything else he values: possessions, relationships, career, and ultimately his very self. On the way down, he manipulates everyone and everything in a losing battle to "keep it all together." In his desperation, he discovers how to coerce friends and family through physical and emotional violence of one kind or another—threatening, lying, blaming, abandonment—and feels increasing contempt for those whom he silences. He avoids those who fight back because they are "dragging him down." And the rest of us, rather than bear the disgust, fear, anger, and shame the addict arouses in us, get away if we can. In the end, the addict is alone, demoralized, sick of life, and wishing he was dead. Small wonder there is such a high suicide rate among alcoholics and addicts.

Taking a more dispassionate view, the emotional dimension of an addiction may be regarded as a *regression* along the line of emotional development. Thus, the alcoholic or addict returns first to feeling and acting like an adolescent, then like a child, and finally, once again, like an infant. This regression doesn't take place overnight, and, once he stops drinking or using, the patient's return to adulthood (or to whatever level of emotional maturity he had reached before he became addicted) also takes time, a process in which professional treatment programs can be very helpful.

By not taking the addict's infantile behavior personally (an almost impossible task for the patient's friends and family), by understanding it as the consequence of his disease and as something he can grow out of, a well-trained and experienced clinical staff can forgive some pretty awful behavior while at the same time not condoning it. By seeing clear limits set on behavior and compliance required with the rules of the treatment program (no violence or threats of violence, no using, etc.), the recovering alcoholic or addict isn't rejected out of hand and has a chance to relearn the fundamental rules of living among other people. He can begin the arduous task of growing up again and, with any luck, will become emotionally capable of participating in 12-step work.

For a treatment staff, this means learning one of the great lessons of psychotherapy: knowing the feelings of another by becoming aware of them in yourself. If you are starting out reasonably "clean" (without chronic negativity of your own), then the feelings you begin to experience in an intense relationship with a patient are usually a direct reflection of the patient's feelings. Of course, this *if* is enormous, because unless the therapist is utterly silent and unseen, it is impossible not to project at least some of your own personal history and values onto the relationship, especially in the face of patients who repeatedly relapse, miss appointments, and refuse to try what you have suggested.

Nevertheless, when counseling works well, a skilled therapist can take the patient's emotional "temperature" by noting his or her own feelings. If you become angry with a patient who seems the very picture of compliance, chances are pretty good that patient is seething inside. If a patient's dramatic display of sadness leaves you unaffected, it's probably because it isn't genuine. And so on.

Therapeutic relationships also inevitably evoke in patients the same feelings patients had toward authority figures in childhood, especially toward their parents. Psychoanalysts call this phenomenon *transference*; the patient "transfers" feelings from the past to the therapist. And, in a corresponding manner (*called countertransference*), the therapist's feelings toward the patient often reflect what the patient's parents felt toward him.

I've come to think of all these feelings literally as the patient's own emotional "stuff" being transmitted to and received (temporarily, we hope) by us. If we can accept all this material, contain it, and help the patient become aware of it, then he has a chance of changing his behavior, of not acting only from impulse but of thinking through the source of his feelings and considering the consequences of his choices.

A note of caution for treatment providers: Often, especially at the beginning of treatment, addicts and alcoholics arouse feelings in us that are too intense to handle by oneself. Group therapy in a program setting, conducted by an interdisciplinary team, is the safest and most effective form of psychotherapy with addicts and alcoholics in early recovery.

In order to grow in self-awareness, addicted patients need to be able to share highly shameful thoughts and feelings. They need to have the experience of speaking their minds both with and without worrying about how it affects others and whether or not it is appropriate. They need to learn how to ask for advice and how to evaluate the advice they receive. Above all, they need to learn to trust others and to be trusted in return. Well-run group therapy is an ideal setting for learning these lessons.

If group therapy is successful, patients can make significant progress toward restoring genuine self-esteem and undermining the false self-love of narcissism. They become less judgmental and more forgiving by learning to put themselves in the place of another. They learn to value open and honest expression of what they do and don't want rather than to deceptively manipulate others for secret purposes. All this is excellent preparation for participating openly and honestly in a 12-step group.

In addition to individual and group therapy for the addict or alcoholic, treatment will almost always include family therapy as well. The families of addicts and alcoholics cannot simply walk away, and, as a result, family members go through a series of changes that parallel the emotional regression of the alcoholic or addict himself. Thus, the wife who lies to her husband's supervisor about why he can't come to work today; the husband who learns to turn a deaf ear to his spouse's drunken tirades; the children who pretend not to care when Mom doesn't pick them up after school as she promised to; the parents who feel compelled to search their children's rooms or view their e-mail for evidence of drug use. Just as the primary (or "identified") patient—the addict—changes as a result of becoming dependent on a substance, so too his family, who are dependent on him, develop their own mirror-image set of problems, problems we refer to as "codependence."

Groups of families can be wonderfully effective in helping one another learn to recognize these patterns of feelings, thoughts, and behavior; engage in open and honest communication; and set limits on what they will and will not accept ("tough love"). It can all go a long way toward restoring trust and mutual respect and in addition prepares family members to become active, dedicated members of their own 12-step and support groups: Al-Anon, Families Anonymous, Codependents Anonymous, Adult Children of Alcoholics, and so on.

THE DIMENSIONS OF
TREATMENT: COGNITIVE

At the beginning of recovery, most alcoholics and addicts don't know how to think about what's wrong with them. Much of what they do think is distorted by denial but not all of it. Through lectures, reading assignments, videos, and discussion groups, patients can learn how to think about what an addiction is and how to deal with it. Perhaps the most important of all these lessons is learning the difference between behavior and illness, between doing something that many people do (drinking) and having something that only some people get (the automatism). When this understanding takes root, the stigma of being an alcoholic or addict is diminished, and patients become clear about what they are and are not responsible for. They begin to see that abstinence is only the beginning of recovery and that the enduring task is learning how not to start up again. All this relieves unnecessary guilt and helps people to focus their energies on present tasks rather than to endlessly regret the past.

THE DIMENSIONS OF
TREATMENT: SPIRITUAL

Once more: It is a simple fact that thousands of people have recovered from addiction through 12-step programs. It is also a fact that, however they define it, members of 12-step groups identify a spiritual awakening as the key to their recovery. This puts many treatment professionals, especially those who are not in recovery themselves, in a difficult position. Most of us were taught that treatment ought to be grounded in science, not faith. Even if a therapist is sympathetic to the idea of spirituality, few have had any serious training in these matters. As a result, many therapists have little spiritual guidance to offer and only their own personal experiences to share, something most of us were rigorously trained *not* to do.

Many addiction treatment programs solve this problem by including pastoral counseling in the care they provide, but for the vast majority of alcoholics and addicts who receive treatment only from a physician, a counselor, or some other health-care professional, the problem remains. I'm only going to touch briefly on it here, because the question of what spirituality means and what it has to do with recovery from addiction is the main theme of the next chapter.

A really serious illness, an illness that brings a human being face to face with his mortality, ought to raise the most important questions anyone can ask himself: Who am I? Why am I alive? Does my life matter? The addictive disorders are unique among serious illnesses in that recovery demands a response to these questions. Either you face them or you don't. Both choices have consequences, and there is no third option. Why?

Recovery from addiction means choosing not to drink or use again. Insofar as an addict or alcoholic wants to stop the painful consequences of the addiction, he will make that choice. As long as he finds some happiness in abstinence and remembers the pain of drinking or using, he'll continue to make that choice. So far, so good. No need to look beyond what Freud called the "pleasure principle" and what behaviorists label as "positive and negative reinforcements." No need for anything spiritual yet.

Here's the rub: If virtually everything that makes you happy can be taken away or lost, perhaps even for reasons having nothing to do with your addiction, then why take on the hard choices? Why spend all the time and effort to "take life on life's terms," as it is said in AA, if you're going to suffer anyway? If all your relationships will wax and wane in happiness and disappointment, why sacrifice for them? If all your accomplishments are likely to be forgotten as the generations pass, why labor for them? If we are all going to become sick and die in the end, why *not* blot out the suffering now? If life has no purpose beyond mere physical survival, if it is merely a succession of pains and pleasures followed by oblivion, then why stay sober for it? Why *not* get loaded? And here, medical science stands silent.

The really big question—the real eight-hundred-pound gorilla in the living room of addiction treatment—is not *how* people stay sober but *why*. It's not that medical or psychological treatment doesn't help people cope with the consequences of an addiction; it's that treatment based on science alone gives no compelling reason to accept the inescapable suffering of simply being alive.

If I stay sober to save my marriage, for example, what happens if my wife dies or leaves me? If I stay sober to keep my job, what happens if I'm fired or when I retire? If I quit for my children, what happens when they grow up and leave home? If I quit to regain my health, what happens if I lose it to some other illness through no fault of my own?

Mere abstinence is a shaky foundation for recovery because without *recovery*, without a sense of what suffering is for, abstinence is simply self-denial, wanting to drink or use but not doing it. It's commendable and even necessary, but it's only the beginning, only flipping the switch of the automatism to the "off" position. Although it is required for recovery, abstinence alone—abstinence without the sense that suffering has a meaning—is sooner or later likely to become unbearable.

When an alcoholic or addict begins to understand that suffering is not only inevitable but essential for discovering the purpose of human life and consciousness, then he's begun to move beyond mere abstinence and into true recovery. As C. S. Lewis put it in *The Problem of Pain*, suffering "is [God's] megaphone to a deaf world." To embark on the spiritual dimension of recovery means facing what it means to be a human being, taking on age-old questions we should all be asking ourselves, questions it is foolish to put off until answering them becomes an urgent necessity.

WHY CAN'T MEDICAL SCIENCE "CURE" ADDICTION?

There is always an easy solution to every human problem—neat, plausible and wrong.

—H. L. MENCKEN

Several years ago, the California Society of Addiction Medicine presented a workshop called Spirituality in Addiction Medicine. But even before the workshop began, an angry member sent a highly critical letter to the governing board. He wasn't upset merely with a particular aspect of the program but with the fact that we were doing it at all. As he put it, "Why is addiction medicine the only specialty which depends on 'divine intervention' for a cure?"

To me, this physician's sarcasm reflected a gross misunderstanding of AA's concept of a Higher Power as well as an astonishing ignorance of the history of his own profession. The former, though regrettable, is perhaps understandable; the latter, inexcusable.

Throughout the long history of medicine, nearly all physicians have had faith in some kind of Higher Power, however they may have conceived of it. One of the greatest surgeons of all time, Ambroise Paré, the man who *invented* the technique of tying off bleeding vessels (instead of burning them, as was standard practice), spoke for all thoughtful physicians when he said: "I merely dress the wound, God heals it."

It's easy to see how my angry colleague came to his pride in self-sufficiency. Imagine that he's called to the emergency room to examine a patient with a fever and the sudden onset of abdominal pain. He correctly diagnoses an inflamed appendix and performs the lifesaving operation. A few days later the patient is up and around, the wound is healing nicely, and there are no complications. The patient has survived what could have been a fatal illness. Obviously, the doctor effected the cure, right? If the assumption were questioned, the doctor would probably respond, "Of course I cured him! Who made the diagnosis? Who performed the surgery? Some ghostly 'Higher Power'? No! I did it. We don't need divine intervention. Scientific progress is the answer to all that mumbo jumbo."

Now, if your concept of a Higher Power is that of a bearded grandfather sitting on a throne in space, then the idea of divine intervention is absurd. But that's a child's conception of a Higher Power. Serious-minded people of faith understand that all human conceptions about a Higher Power are inadequate, especially those based on picture thinking. Thinking seriously about a Higher Power can begin with recognizing that such a being may actually work through other human beings. For most physicians, including my surgeon friend, that simple idea should lead to a sense of gratitude for all the men and women who labored so hard to give us the practice of medicine we have today.

From gratitude to our predecessors, we progress to gratitude for creation itself. Hence, the next step in thinking about a Higher Power is to realize that the body's capacity to restore itself is part of something much larger than our operations and medications. It's a part of the whole flow of life on Earth, a living current that stretches back over billions of years to an origin we do not know. Modern medicine does indeed work wonders but only because we are a part of that current. Cut off from it, we don't even exist. We are not omnipotent, and, contrary to my angry colleague's belief in endless progress, the proof lies in our inability to "cure" addictions.

This idea that medical science should be able to cure addiction was wonderfully (if crudely) expressed to me one day by a patient at one of my weekly lectures. The man was unhappy with a whole variety of things and took advantage of my invitation for questions to blast me with it:

> "Say, Doc, if addiction is a disease, how come you
> guys haven't come up with a cure for it? You can

put new hearts in people and do all kinds of stuff.
Why haven't you got something for us alcoholics?"

"Well, let me ask you a question first," I responded.
"If we were to come up with such a treatment,
what would it do? I mean, how would it affect you?"

"That's easy!" he shot back. "It'd make me not want
to drink!"

I answered, "Oh, well, we've had that for a long time.
It's called Valium. If you take enough Valium, you
won't want to drink, I guarantee it."

After an uneasy silence, the other patients saw past my poker face and began to laugh. But it had taken them a long moment to realize that my idea for "treatment" was no cure. It was simply replacing one addiction with another. And, in any case, the patient didn't really want to be rid of his desire to drink. He wanted to be able to drink like a nonalcoholic: without the automatism starting up and running his life. He didn't want to quit drinking; he wanted to be able to get away with it.

The patient is not to be blamed for his attitude. The idea of a cure for addiction has been promoted and defended by medical and scientific experts for a long time. Most recently (2008), Dr. Nora Volkow, the director of the National Institute on Drug Abuse, was quoted by *Newsweek* magazine as saying, "In ten years we will be treating addiction as a disease, and that means with medicine." But this claim is nothing new. In 1990, Dr. Ernest Noble, a highly respected UCLA professor and prominent brain researcher said the same thing. His optimistic prediction appeared in a letter to the *Los Angeles Times*:

> Now, for the first time, biomedical science may be capable of providing us the tools to reverse addiction, permitting us to cure and rehabilitate the afflicted. Advances in molecular and cellular biology have brought us to the point where we can understand the underlying basis of addiction and learn to alter brain cells to eliminate the cravings that permanently victimize the user. . . .
>
> Ten to fifteen years of a well-funded commitment should elucidate the detailed mechanisms underlying each of the principal addictions. Treatments could be designed to reverse the long-term cellular changes. Both the acute drug effects and the persistent cravings that lock addicts into their habits would be reversible immediately. . . .

As of this writing, it's been nearly twenty years since Dr. Noble wrote this letter, and while there have been some very interesting discoveries in brain science, nothing fundamental has changed in the medical treatment of addiction. Of course, these promises are very attractive, especially to addicts and alcoholics who don't want to have to work at recovery. They also make good newspaper copy and build demand for more research. Dr. Noble's knowledge of brain physiology and biochemistry was wonderful, and I know from personal experience that his intentions were utterly honorable, but I don't think he'd spent nearly enough time talking to addicts and alcoholics about what they actually experience.

There already exists, for example, a drug (naltrexone) that blocks the "high" after an addict injects heroin or morphine. From a neurochemical point of view, it's a brilliant treatment. If the addict gets no effect, there's no point in using. All very logical. The trouble is that very few people will take naltrexone voluntarily for long. Why? Most often, because they want to get high again, and this not so much because they are victims of an irresistible craving but because they are bored, lonely, angry, hurt, or just want to "party." In the absence of finding any new meaning in life, there is simply no enduring reason *not* to use again. Most of the people for whom naltrexone has proven useful are health-care professionals threatened with the loss of licensure if they use narcotics again. None that I've treated wanted to continue taking it once that threat had passed.

The whole idea of addiction as a curable condition is a result of not understanding what it is, of conceiving of addiction as disordered behavior rather than as a disease of automaticity. This misunderstanding leads naturally to a second error: failing to recognize that quitting and relapsing are two entirely different problems that belong to two utterly different levels of human life. The first is material; the second, spiritual. Although these two levels are related, they simply cannot be approached as if they were the same.

At the material (or biochemical) level, the idea of a cure makes sense, as in the treatment of withdrawal syndromes. But at the spiritual level, recovery from addiction doesn't depend on fixing abnormal brain chemistry but rather on the addict's willingness to take on difficult choices. The proof is obvious: Drugs that are claimed to prevent relapse (after withdrawal is over), only "work" as long as the patient *wants* to remain abstinent. Wanting to remain abstinent requires the willingness to face at least some suffering as the price of change. What sort of drug could give anyone that? Do medical scientists imagine that they can package *meaning* in a pill? Certainly, chemistry can supply temporary relief from craving, sedation, tranquilization, even energy. But understanding, courage, selflessness?

The drug disulfiram (Antabuse) provides another example in the long, misguided search for an alcoholism cure. It is a deterrent—that is, it makes people sick if they drink while taking it. If the patient is coerced or desperate, he will take the drug and probably won't risk getting sick by drinking. But once the coercion is gone, once the patient isn't so desperate, continuing to take Antabuse begins to seem ridiculous. At that point, if the patient decides he wants to drink again, he simply stops taking the pill and waits a few days.

It is claimed that other drugs decrease cravings. Such medications may indeed be useful at the beginning of sobriety, but if the patient simply remains abstinent, cravings usually die away on their own. At that point, why would anyone take a drug to get rid of something they're not experiencing? No one keeps taking aspirin once the headache is gone. Several years ago, for example, there was a brief flurry of interest in the drug bromocriptine (Parlodel) which, it was hoped, would decrease cocaine craving. But well-conducted studies failed to show any long-term benefit. There's no great mystery about it. Most cocaine addicts who have been clean for several months (and many have been) report that they didn't start up again because they were craving the drug. They began again because they believed that if they used, they wouldn't lose control again. If they did believe it, then they used because they were already so miserable that they didn't care what would happen when they did.

Some newer drugs that reportedly decrease craving for alcohol simply haven't stood the test of time. Acamprosate (Campral), for example, won FDA approval on the basis of studies conducted over relatively brief periods of time: twelve weeks to six months. Much the same is true of studies conducted on naltrexone (Revia), reputed to reduce the pleasure of drinking. Only the pharmaceutical companies promote these drugs with any great enthusiasm. Most clinicians and scientists who actually work with alcoholics and addicts for significant periods of time are all too aware that drug treatment alone (without counseling, "psychosocial support," or AA) doesn't work in the long run.

There is one exception to the futility of treating addiction with drugs alone, and, like all exceptions, it proves the rule. The strictly medical treatment of opiate addiction does convey long-term benefits but at a price. Drugs such as methadone and buprenorphine (Subutex) eliminate the craving for heroin, morphine, oxycodone, and so on, but it's because they are longer-acting drugs of the same kind. In fact, they are hardly less addictive than the illicit drugs they replace. They are useful primarily because they are legal, not because they "cure" the addiction. Patients can remain on them indefinitely without having to resort to drug dealers, black-market prices, and doing all the things it takes to pay those prices. That freedom gives opiate addicts a chance to put their lives back together, but getting off these prescribed opiates can be every bit as difficult as quitting the original, illicit drug. And even if patients do manage to become entirely drug free, without some new capacity to find meaning in suffering, they're just as likely to turn to some other form of intoxication for relief from unhappiness and then to become addicted to that.

Medical science, however, is nothing if not persistent. Dr. Charles O'Brien, an otherwise thoughtful and accomplished psychiatrist, wrote this in an editorial for the *American Journal of Psychiatry*:

> Perhaps one of the reasons that medications are not routinely used to prevent alcohol relapse lies in the notion that total abstinence is the only desirable goal and a medication that blocks some of the rewarding properties of alcohol is dismissed as a "crutch."

Citing the "biological basis" of alcoholism, he concludes that "perhaps a crutch is medically and morally justified."

To be sure, a crutch is a great thing if you have a broken leg, but if you refuse to participate in a program of rehabilitation after the bone has healed (because the crutch enables you to get around despite the injury), then what was once helpful becomes an obstacle to recovery. Obviously, this is rarely a problem for someone with a broken leg, because virtually everyone with such an injury *wants* to walk normally again. But this is not the case for many alcoholics and addicts.

After withdrawal is over, it is far less the "rewarding effects" of alcohol that drive the patient to drink again and much more the absence of any better rewards for staying sober, rewards the addict could only come to by accepting suffering as an inescapable part of the transformation we call recovery. The beginning of recovery almost always means facing up to disasters: health problems, divorce, unemployment, alienation from friends and family. Only someone who is convinced that there is no other way out is willing to face it all as the price of change.

Contrary to Dr. O'Brien's opinion, total abstinence isn't the foundation of recovery from addiction for doctrinaire reasons. It is the goal of treatment because, for an addict, "having just one" sooner or later leads to having another, which, in turn, leads to reinstatement of the automatism and eventually to a full relapse. And where, when, and how that relapse will end, no one knows.

I sometimes wonder if the professionals who believe that a life of sustained moderation is possible for addicts and alcoholics are mistakenly applying lessons learned at the level of social or public health to the level of individual patients. Reducing the overall quantity of alcohol or drugs consumed by a population is beneficial, and to the degree that some social engineering results in a decreased prevalence of drug- and alcohol-related problems, then it's a good thing. Even though the "great experiment" of Prohibition failed to impose abstinence on a large population, it did decrease the rates of cirrhosis.

But these kinds of solutions, what may be called the "quantitative" or "statistical" approach to addiction, simply don't translate as goals for individual alcoholics and addicts. For an alcoholic, fewer drinking days and less alcohol consumed per drinking episode may be helpful in the short run, but they just don't hold up over the long haul. Alcoholism isn't characterized by the quantity or frequency of drinking but by its nature and consequences. Being a little less intoxicated on any given day makes no difference, if, as a result of being intoxicated at all, you crash your car into a school bus full of children.

Again, at the beginning of recovery, alcoholics and addicts may well need medical help to stop using the addictive substance. At that stage, the biologically driven urge to drink or use can be overwhelming, and quitting without medical help may even be dangerous. This is the biological level of addiction to which Drs. Noble, Volkow, and O'Brien refer and for which medication may be critically important. But the longer the addict remains abstinent, especially if he becomes an active member of a 12-step group, the more these kinds of biologically driven urges die away. If they return, they are almost always the result of fundamental *psychological* processes: conditioned reflexes and/or the desire to escape emotional distress. At that point, treating these urges as if they were purely *biological* processes is absurd. What sort of medication could wipe out the impulse to escape suffering and yet also leave the patient's emotional life intact? Isn't that precisely the kind of drug that leads to addiction in the first place? And even if such a thing were possible, the addiction itself—the automatism—would still be a permanent part of the patient's brain. Like all automatisms, it can't be eliminated; it can only be made dormant. If engaged, it will once again spring to life.

I suppose medical scientists might try to devise a treatment that selectively eliminates only one automatism while leaving all the other useful ones (e.g., reading, walking, talking) un-affected. It seems highly unlikely that such a project could suc-ceed. Of course, if the addict's urges to drink or to use are made more difficult because he has an additional medical or psychi-atric condition (e.g., chronic pain, depression) and if there is a safe treatment for that condition, then medication (such as an antidepressant) may be both important and helpful. But deciding when a patient's suffering is due to such an illness and not simply part of the human condition is not so easy. It requires all the skill and patience a clinician can muster, and, in any case, the patient still needs to be clean and sober. For the purposes of this argument, it is sufficient to point out that in seeking to "cure" addiction, medical science is making the fundamental mistake of failing to distinguish between that suffering which is pathological and that which must be trans-formed for recovery.

To achieve and maintain abstinence, an addict has to make difficult choices. Acting on those choices means making sacri-fices. Making sacrifices means suffering. And suffering forces the addict to ask what his suffering is *for*, what it *means*. If it means nothing, then, at some point, after the difficulties of quit-ting are over, there will be no good reason not to drink or use again. No medicine, no passively received treatment will ever produce that understanding. Recovery is work.

For the recovering alcoholic or addict, understanding the meaning of suffering begins with acceptance or, as it is put in AA, "surrender." Surrender does not mean passive acquiescence to any and all suffering. It means a hard-won change of attitude that makes it possible to distinguish between the suffering that is of our own making and can be overcome and that which is inescapable and essential for spiritual development.

The great Stoic philosopher Epictetus said it about as simply as it can be said: "Some things are up to us and some things are not up to us." Without the capacity to know this difference, all suffering will be merely something to be gotten rid of. Its meaning will be lost, and the wish to be sober will be at the mercy of events that neither the addict nor his doctor can do anything about.

SUMMING UP

By way of summarizing the relationship between treatment and recovery, let me offer this analogy. Imagine I've put a seed in your hand. Now I'd like to ask you a question. Can you *make* it grow?

I hope you are at least a little puzzled by my having italicized the word *make*. I wanted to make you pause, to make you think, in case you might be tempted to respond habitually "Yes, of course." Because unless you think about it, you're likely to see a seed only as a particular thing occupying a particular place at a particular moment. Looking only with your eyes, you don't see the long history that led up to it: the generations of ancestors, the soil and water and sun that nourished that lineage, the whole infinite stretch of time and space of which life on Earth is a part.

If you keep just a little of that in your mind's eye, you will realize that you don't make the seed grow. What you *can* do is plant it, water it, fertilize it, keep the bugs away, and so on. In short, you can cultivate it. When you do those things reasonably skillfully, the seed probably will sprout, grow to maturity, and, in its turn, produce more seeds like itself. But to suppose that you make that happen is at best ignorant and at worst delusional.

The seed is recovery. The water, fertilizer, bug spray, and so on, are maintaining abstinence, participating in 12-step meetings, obtaining a sponsor, working on the steps, and so on. Growth doesn't come from us; it comes from something inherent in the seed. It comes, as AA teaches, from something well beyond you and me. If you like, it comes from God. If you don't like, it comes from a Higher Power, from Nature, from five billion years of the evolution of life on Earth, from the created universe, from whatever you want to call it.

Translated to the treatment of an alcoholic or addict, the lesson is that none of us—not me, not family, friends, employers, colleagues, nor judges—makes anyone recover. Strangely, even the patient himself can't command the spiritual awakening needed for an enduring recovery from addiction.

Some seeds are so robust that they flourish without much apparent effort on the part of the gardener. They just seem to land in the right spot at the right time. Others land in much less fertile soil. Some are eaten by birds or washed away. And sadly, some are so badly damaged as to be incapable of growth. The parable of the sower in the New Testament says it eloquently (Mark 4:1–20).

Even if the seed of recovery does take root, not all aspects of growth are so rosy. In fact, it all bears a remarkable resemblance to the stages of death and dying as formulated by the late Elisabeth Kübler-Ross: denial, anger, bargaining, depression, and, finally, acceptance. This last stage—acceptance (or "surrender," as it was termed by Dr. Harry Tiebout)—marks the death of the old ways of thinking and acting that supported the addiction. Without it, recovery is never secure. Again, as it is recorded in the New Testament, "Except a corn of wheat fall into the ground and die, it abideth alone: but if it die, it bringeth forth much fruit" (John 12:24).

Many addicts and alcoholics become good gardeners "naturally," that is to say, they find the 12-step programs on their own and proceed to work at them effectively. But a substantial number of others do not. Or, alternatively, the people who care about them may not want to wait to see if their loved one finds the 12-steps in time. In either case, these are the people who come for professional help because they haven't found the 12-steps on their own.

Professional treatment isn't a substitute for the growth that comes with participation in a 12-step program. Rather, it is a sort of incubator or greenhouse which is sometimes necessary to get the process of growth started. Once the seedling is capable of sustaining itself, it comes out of the artificial environment and begins to make its way in the natural world.

In summary, then, and once more, the goal of treatment is to help patients overcome obstacles to becoming dedicated, active members of a 12-step group. And that means, in the long run, helping people toward a spiritual awakening.

Chapter Four

IS A SPIRITUAL
AWAKENING NECESSARY
FOR RECOVERY?

SOME DEFINITIONS

When I first began working with alcoholics and addicts, I had no idea that there was anything spiritual about Alcoholics Anonymous or recovery from addiction. I don't think my ignorance harmed any of the patients I was taking care of then. Most were in the very first stages of recovery and didn't need to think much about spiritual questions. At that point, they were simply trying to make it through withdrawal, and my job was to help them do it. It was only later, when treatment shifted to rehabilitation, that matters of the spirit became important. It was then, too, that the demon of definitions reared its head.

I have often wished that we had some word other than *spiritual* to describe the opening of heart and mind that enables people to stay sober despite all the things life throws at them. The word *spiritual* has been so overused that it's lost much of its value as a way of referring to the great questions of human existence and a transcendent reality. Not long ago, after I suggested to a patient that she might benefit from having a spiritual practice in her life, she responded indignantly that she already did—she read her horoscope every day without fail! I could hardly believe she thought that's what I had in mind, and I had to work hard to find some other word to convey what I meant. I'm still looking, so until I find something better I'll continue to use the overwrought and much-abused *spiritual*.

Also, I still want to keep things simple, and that has raised the problem of not sounding like a lunatic. Anyone who claims to have a simple answer to the purpose and meaning of human life will persuade only the most gullible and is probably headed for some kind of fundamentalism to boot. The religious forms of fundamentalism are well known, but there are others— political, philosophical, and even medical. I have no interest in contributing to any of them. And yet it seems undeniable that a durable recovery from addiction depends on a sense that human life has some meaning beyond mere physical survival. Twenty-five years of clinical practice has convinced me that without at least a hint of that meaning, the alcoholic or addict who is *merely* abstinent is at significant risk of relapse under the onslaught of injustice, misfortune, or simply the erosive effects of time itself.

Before going further, however, some definitions are in order. First, the word *meaning*, then *spiritual*, and finally *recovery*.

MEANING

In its simplest sense, a thing has meaning insofar as it stands for something other than itself. The ink marks forming the words of this sentence have meaning only because they call up particular ideas in the reader's mind. Inked chicken scratchings would have no such meaning, except perhaps to a farmer or ornithologist and then not because the bird intended it. In the same way, then, for life (and the suffering that comes with it) to have meaning, it must signify something else. It must point to something beyond itself. But what could be beyond life, beyond nature?

The conventional, nonspiritual response to this question rests on the assumption that life can be defined purely in biological terms. Thus, it is said that an individual human life has meaning insofar as it is part of the greater life of humanity or of life as a whole. For most people that means all the customary goals that bring a sense of purpose to daily life: securing the health and well-being of our families, friends, and community; useful work; artistic creativity; recreational pursuits; and so on. All contribute in some way to the community of human beings, something that is beyond any particular individual life, whether or not we intend anything about it.

On one level, this response to the question of meaning makes sense but not much more for you or me than it does for an ant. And, indeed, in the view of many modern scientists, human beings are simply a very advanced kind of animal. From the strictly biological point of view, human beings are different from other animals, including ants, only insofar as we have *more* of what they also have: more social interaction, more capacity for communication, more consciousness, and so on. But this application of the idea of meaning isn't really pointing to something *beyond* life itself; it's only pointing to *more* life, more of the same. *Beyond* life means something *other than* biological life, and therefore it means something that cannot be known through the senses, the organs of life.

SPIRITUAL

In thinking about the definition of *meaning* in this way, a simple definition of the word *spiritual* suggests itself: the dimension of human life that cannot be perceived through the senses and that gives a unique meaning to each individual human life.

When we are related to this dimension, our lives point to something beyond all the goals given by life itself—the satisfaction of our appetites and ambitions, our efforts on behalf of our families, neighbors, and communities—more even than the wish to leave something beneficial for posterity. None of these purposes is incompatible with the spiritual dimension, but none of them requires it. An act of responsibility, charity, or forgiveness may or may not be accompanied by spiritual awareness. On the other hand, a truly spiritual nature will strive to be responsible, charitable, and forgiving. It will also know when it has fallen short.

RECOVERY

Following from these definitions of *meaning* and *spirituality*, then, *recovery* doesn't mean simply that the alcoholic or drug addict has become abstinent or even that he's resumed the activities of daily life—that is, work, family, recreation. The idea of recovery suggested here means, first, that an addict or alcoholic realizes that he belongs to something greater than himself and, second, that he is willing to try to act in accordance with that realization, especially when only a memory of it remains and life seems unbearable.

It may be argued that including the spiritual dimension in a definition of recovery is unnecessary and perhaps even unfair. After all, many addicts and alcoholics modify their use or even abstain for quite long periods without any sort of spiritual awakening and without becoming active members of a 12-step program (or any other spiritually based community). I would reply that each case has to be examined individually.

In the first place, many people who get into some trouble with drugs or alcohol and who subsequently moderate their use were not addicted. They may never be. They did not experience the irresistible craving, obsession, and compulsion for which abstinence is the only reliable solution. Quitting or cutting down temporarily isn't the test of addiction. The test is whether or not drinking or using again reawakens what abstinence had made dormant. Those who have had problems with drugs or alcohol but who never became addicted—who don't have the automatism of addiction—may have no more need for a spiritual awakening than a person who never had any kind of problem with drugs or alcohol at all. For all these people, suffering doesn't automatically awaken the urge to escape through intoxication. For the truly addicted, however, even though they may be abstinent, it is a very different story.

For true alcoholics and addicts who have only quit (i.e., who are not engaged in the work of recovery), any sort of pain—physical, emotional, or mental—triggers the reminder that intoxication is a quick and efficient way out. The addict may or may not choose to act on that reminder, but the fact that it comes up is part of the automatism. With the growth of recovery, the addict learns that the promise of relief through intoxication is an illusion. He learns that suffering may be put off but that it does not go away. It's a lesson that takes both time and effort. As a result, the newly or merely abstinent addict carries two burdens: first, the suffering that triggered the urge to escape and, second, all the difficulties inherent in not acting on that urge.

Perhaps this is why *mere* abstinence—abstinence without recovery—so often seems such an unhappy, begrudging thing. The alcoholic may be "dry," the addict "clean," without recovery, but there is no restoration of a fully human life with its successes and failures, joys and sorrows, acceptance and forgiveness. Instead, there is the gray rigidity of a life lived by the "safety first" policy, a sense that the addict has put himself in a behavioral box with little room for all the risks inherent in a life fully lived. Some nominal members of 12-step groups even do the same. Still, I don't want to be rigid about it myself. Addicts and alcoholics who are merely abstinent are almost always better off and causing less trouble than if they had continued to drink or use drugs. Their abstinence may be a brittle achievement, but I wouldn't want to say anything that makes it more difficult for them to maintain it.

Defining recovery in this way and suggesting that it requires a spiritual awakening raise questions that go well beyond the problems of drug and alcohol addiction, problems that are at the very core of human nature itself.

ADDICTION: A NEW METAPHOR
FOR HUMAN SUFFERING

So far, I've been writing about the problem of addiction in its strictly medical sense: addiction to drugs and alcohol. Over the last thirty or forty years, however, the idea of addiction has been applied to a much broader range of human problems. The truth is that none of this suffering is new. A hundred years ago, the same problems were thought of as variations on the theme of sin: greed, gluttony, lust, pride, vanity, and so on. Even thinking about them as addictions isn't really new; it's been at the heart of Buddhist teachings since 600 B.C.

I've forgotten where this Zen story comes from, and I apologize for that lapse, but in view of the lesson it teaches I don't think the author will mind if I reproduce it here without personal attribution.

> It seems that a certain Zen priest taught the four noble
> truths of Buddhism:

1. Life is suffering.
2. Suffering is the result of attachment.
3. Attachment is the consequence of illusion—chiefly, the illusion of permanence.
4. Freedom from illusion is enlightenment (awakening).

Now, it came to pass that this priest's son was killed in a horseback-riding accident. Hearing the terrible news, all the pupils rushed to the zendo, where they found their teacher sitting in meditation, tears streaming down his cheeks.

One of the youngest students could not understand why his teacher was weeping and asked him, "Master, why do you grieve? Have you not taught us that all suffering is based on illusion?"

"Yes, it is true," responded the priest, "and the death of a child is the most difficult illusion of all."

I suspect that almost no one, like the Zen master in this story, will ever achieve the sort of freedom from illusion that could transcend the grief of losing a child. Indeed, orthodox Christian doctrine holds that it is impossible, that the human condition is "exile in a vale of tears." As C. S. Lewis puts it (again, through the fictional devil Screwtape), "Suffering is an essential part of what He [God] calls redemption."

Whichever doctrine is correct, it is also true that much of our suffering will be temporary and tolerable. If we rise to it, it can also help make us better people. But some of it will be overwhelming, and then we will seek relief, sometimes from a doctor and his medicines.

The whole thing is summed up neatly in some sage advice I was given when I finished medical school:

> *People go to a doctor for only one of two reasons:*
> *fear or pain.*

My first years of medical practice proved the truth of this pithy remark many times over, but there was a deeper meaning in it that came to me only after several years of working with alcoholics and addicts. Only then did I learn that I wasn't the only doctor to whom people turned when they were afraid or in pain. In fact, in my field (by definition) I was the last. It was only *after* patients had doctored themselves, *after* they had tried and failed to get rid of their fear or pain through drugs and alcohol, that they came to see me.

Some years after that lesson, I learned another one: Drugs and alcohol aren't the only ways people try to escape fear and pain. Anything that provides enough excitement to capture and distract our attention—gambling, pornography, binge eating, shopping, obsessive work, sex as sport, relationships as drama—will divert us from whatever unhappiness we are experiencing at the moment. But these distractions are all only temporary and, as a result, carry with them an even stronger potential for "attachment" (in the sense of the Zen story above) and then of becoming compulsive and destructive addictions.

I didn't fully understand this larger application of the concept of addiction until I attended an Addictions and Consciousness conference in the late 1980s. The presentations and workshops at this conference focused on all kinds of problems people referred to as addictions: love addiction, sex addiction, relationship addiction, possession addiction, power addiction, and others. A whole variety of different 12-step groups were represented at this meeting: Overeaters Anonymous, Gamblers Anonymous, Sex Addicts Anonymous, Emotions Anonymous, Families Anonymous, Debtors Anonymous, and more.

Initially, I confess, I was puzzled and a little skeptical. Why this need to recast old problems in the language of addiction? I had a vague sense that people were reclaiming a way of working on themselves, reasserting their need for a spiritual dimension that they had not received from organized religion and that mental-health professionals weren't offering them. And as I listened to their stories, I began to hear what my drug- and alcohol-addicted patients had been telling me for years: that their lives had become dominated by compulsion and obsession, that abstinence was necessary for recovery, and that a spiritual awakening had put that recovery on a firm foundation.

Eventually, I began to hear the value of the addiction metaphor: Mere abstinence was not enough. The methods of escaping from fear or pain may have been different, but at the heart of each of the 12-step groups was the need to find the meaning of suffering. Without that meaning, there was no enduring reason to stay sober. Suffering awakens the addiction, and it begins to whisper: "You don't have to feel this! Remember me [cocaine, alcohol, heroin, etc.]? You don't have to put up with this. Come on. Here's the way out!"

Sometimes the addict can silence the voice of temptation by

"thinking it through"—that is, by thinking about what's likely to happen if he drinks or uses again, how relapsing would affect his life and the people close to him, and so on. But, in the long run, fear of the merely probable is a poor defense against the guarantee of immediate relief. There are at least three reasons.

First, the capacity to think about potential disaster is up against an inner voice that has all the trappings of reason. It's a part of the mind that has had years of practice, decades devoted to rationalization in service of the addiction (a skill AAs attribute to the disease and describe as "cunning and baffling"). Through it, the addict can convince himself that what has always happened in the past couldn't possibly happen again. Exposing this subtle madness requires the recovering alcoholic to become adept at looking at a drink and seeing that it only *looks* like a drink. In reality, it is *drinking* again. It is his life in ruins: job lost, family gone, health wrecked. A member of AA once expressed it to a group of my students this way: "If I don't have a drink, I can't get drunk. If I don't get drunk, I can't get arrested for drunk driving. If I don't get arrested, I won't lose my job, infuriate my wife, alienate my family . . ."

Second, all the worldly things that an alcoholic or addict stands to lose by drinking or using again are themselves subject to change whether he stays sober or not. By *worldly* (as opposed to *spiritual*) I mean everything that brings temporal happiness: a loving marriage, satisfying work, adoring children, good health, and so on. There isn't anything wrong with enjoying all these things. The problem comes when the alcoholic depends on them as the foundation for abstinence. If, for example, the alcoholic stays sober to keep his marriage, what happens when he's so angry or disappointed with his wife that he wishes he had never met her? Or suppose his doctor has scared him into sobriety with bad news about the state of his liver? What happens six months later when he learns that the organ has repaired itself? Or, again, what if, for reasons having nothing to do with his performance, he loses the job he quit drinking to keep?

The inherent instability of these temporal sources of happiness is well recognized in AA. Relying on them is "making your [wife, husband, job, kids, etc.] your Higher Power." There is a tricky point here: Although you have to treat all of these people and things as though they *belong* to a Higher Power, they are not the Higher Power itself; like you, they are in a continual state of change. One day your wife, your kids, maybe even your boss or clients may love and appreciate you, but the next, they may not. So if you were counting on their constant affection and admiration to keep you happy, you will be sadly disappointed. Disappointment will breed resentment, and soon enough you'll be reminded that intoxication is a quick and reliable way out of the whole mess.

Third, fear is a poor motivation for long-term sobriety because the human organism cannot sustain it. Throughout all the horrors of both natural and man-made disasters, human beings overcome fear in order to go on living. For recovering addicts and alcoholics, it means that the fear that motivates them to quit cannot deliver lasting sobriety. The whole phenomenon is something like a mathematical equation of the emotions. At the moment an addict hits the sort of catastrophe that makes him stop ("bottom" in AA parlance), the fear caused by the addiction is greater than the fear that intoxication was meant to dull.

When that fear fades away and suffering returns, intoxication can begin to look attractive again.

All these problems are addressed by work toward a spiritual awakening, and, in this respect, the recovering alcoholic or drug addict has an advantage over those of us who like to think of ourselves as "normal." The addict knows from bitter experience the unnecessary and meaningless suffering that is in store for him if he relapses. For those of us who haven't struggled with our own perhaps more subtle forms of automaticity with "possession addiction," "relationship addiction," "power addiction," and the like, things aren't necessarily so clear. We don't recognize that all these forms of attachment create an endless cycle of more and more needless suffering.

In any case, spiritual work begins with the possibility of faith, reason in the service of sobriety. Faith is often thought of as irrational, as a function of the emotions: "faith" as a belief in something whose existence cannot be proven. But that is only one meaning. Faith is also one of the theological virtues, and then it isn't empty-headed confidence but a quality of character that requires effort to attain and maintain.

For most alcoholics and addicts, the work of faith is primarily that of remembering what began with "a moment of clarity," a moment of profound certainty that one is headed the wrong way. My AA mentor, Tom Redgate, described what happened to him. In the midst of serving a prison term for crimes committed while drunk, he'd been further confined in solitary for fighting. Then, one morning, out of the blue, he suddenly realized "that I was an 'I,' that what I had become was my own doing and that no one else was to blame." It wasn't a moment he'd sought or worked toward; it was a moment of grace, a higher state of consciousness, the gift of a Higher Power.

Tom never drank again, but he had to work hard to keep the memory of that moment alive. He did that by becoming an active member of AA and dedicating his life to serving his fellow alcoholics. Without his work on the 12 steps, the power of that realization would have faded. Soon enough, he would have begun to blame everyone and everything else for his miseries, and not long thereafter he would have persuaded himself that he had the right to get drunk.

The virtue of faith in a Higher Power also means remembering that we are lower powers. In this sense, having faith puts us in something like the position of a dog who waits patiently outside a building for his master to return. The dog hasn't created the idea of a master out of his own head. He has had the actual experience of being with his master and now waits *in faith* that his master still exists, even though he can't see or hear him at that moment. Having once had a moment of clarity, the experience of a Higher Power, the recovering alcoholic or addict is in the same situation: waiting faithfully for what he once knew with certainty to be true.

Working toward a spiritual awakening, then, means putting what faith you have in the right place. Unlike anything or anyone else you might get sober for, a Higher Power doesn't change. Later in this chapter I'll offer some ideas for pondering that, but for now the gist of it is contained in the idea that a Higher Power is eternal. Nothing else is. Relationships, health, satisfaction with work, the joys of creativity and recreation—all are subject to change. That's why depending on them as a foundation for sobriety is a mistake. Eventually, at least for some period of time, all of them will stop making us happy. At some point, they will even be the source of frustration and disappointment.

The third step of AA, like all the world's great spiritual teachings, indicates the corrective measure:

> *Made a decision to turn our will and our lives over to the*
> *care of God, as we understood him.*

Please note some critical wording here. It doesn't say "turned our will and our lives over to God." It says "to the *care of* God." Since, by definition, we don't know what the care of a Higher Power, a greater intelligence, might mean for us, we are not to wait passively in the expectation that we will be given what we think we need—however desperately we may wish it. The third step teaches that grace will come. How and where, we do not know. Meanwhile, we have our work.

Like all the others, step three is never really finished, and nothing is more effective at providing the opportunity to remember the presence of a Higher Power than being with other recovering alcoholics and addicts. The 12-step fellowships provide those opportunities in abundance. Self-absorption and self-concern are in direct opposition to remembering that you are under the care of a Higher Power. Doing the work of "getting out of self"—being of service to others (the twelfth step)—strengthens faith and brings a joy that transcends the emotional ups and downs of daily life. Even in the midst of profound sadness, there can be a deep gratitude for being sober to experience it.

There may be enlightened beings somewhere who live in continual consciousness of a Higher Power. I don't know of any, but I do know that the rest of us are subject to forgetfulness. That's the bad news. The good news is that when we remember and choose to work in obedience to that memory, a feeling far beyond any temporary happiness begins to grow. In the end, it becomes an unshakable foundation for sobriety.

WHY A NEW METAPHOR?

I suspect that the appearance of addiction as a metaphor for suffering is simply one more reflection of a profound change in many of the institutions that once transmitted traditional values from one generation to the next. All those values had to do with what it means to become a good or virtuous person (virtue: αρετή, or *arete*, in the ancient Greek, meaning "excellence"). These days, hardly anyone has even heard of the cardinal virtues—temperance, prudence, justice, and fortitude—let alone understands and values them. No doubt, the theological virtues of faith, hope, and love must seem hopelessly old-fashioned to most moderns. What happened?

It does seem that twenty-first-century American life is substantially different from what it was in previous eras. In the brief span of seventy-five years or so, the United States has gone from being an agrarian, family-centered, and isolated nation to being an urban, multicultural, postindustrial member of a "global village." Virtually all of our families came from somewhere else, and, for most, the traditions that provided a sense of community in the old country did not last long here.

By and large, the inculcation of values in children has been turned over to educational systems that are neither equipped nor designed to teach what children ought to be learning at home. The influence of television and electronic entertainment in general—fast-paced, compelling impressions received by a largely passive and uncritical audience—has created an unprecedented separation between feelings and actions. Even higher education has succumbed to the pressures of the modern industrial-information state: college and university students increasingly bent on "getting a degree" rather than receiving something that might help them wonder at their own existence.

Perhaps it is not so strange then that video, TV, and Internet-stimulated children become the young adults who turn, almost without hesitation, to ready-made escapes from loneliness, boredom, and fear. Without effective guidance based on traditional and spiritual values, they have few alternatives but to plunge headlong into all those things that can become addictions: drugs and alcohol, overeating, gambling, promiscuity, obsessive exercise, drama-filled relationships, shopping sprees, compulsive work, and so on.

None of these attempts to avoid suffering works in the long run. Like it or not, suffering really is inescapable, and, in time, what was at first an easy way out stops working. The dose, whether it be that of a drug, of excitement, of praise, of the feeling of belonging, or of mere distraction, has to be increased to have an effect. In the end, repetition dulls the senses and escape becomes impossible. Meanwhile, the addict has been giving himself the terrible lesson that he has the right to change how he feels whenever and however he wants to.

The addiction metaphor—human beings passively enslaved in automaticity—suits our age perfectly. There is no "them," the addicted, and "us," the normal. To the extent any of us lives in ignorance of the spiritual dimension of our lives—acting automatically without any sense of obligation to something or someone beyond ourselves—then we too are addicted. The doctor who buries himself in work to avoid the disappointment of an unhappy marriage is fundamentally no different from the salesman who drinks to numb the humiliation of a job that disgusts him, or from the compulsive jogger who runs away from confronting her undisciplined children, or from the self-made martyr who tolerates her abusive, drug-addicted husband rather than face her own sense of worthlessness. It is simply that some addictions are more easily recognized and less socially acceptable than others because the damage is more obvious and appears sooner.

Faced with the undeniable value of 12-step work in recovery from addiction, many otherwise well-meaning psychologists and psychiatrists have tried to get rid of the troubling "Higher Power" business by attributing the benefits of AA to psychological mechanisms: group identification, the ventilation of feelings, and so on. No doubt all these mechanisms are at work, but by focusing on them and excluding the influence of a Higher Power, we lose the forest for the trees, miss the essence for the details. It's as though, after hearing Beethoven's Ninth Symphony, an electrician tried to "explain" how it affected you by describing how the radio worked. Yes, of course, all those physical facts are quite real and even very interesting, but don't then reduce the "Ode to Joy" to mere electronics! They are simply not the same level of phenomenon. We live in two worlds: one that is material, tangible, quantitative, phenomenal; the other, spiritual, intangible, qualitative, noumenal. Both are valid and related, but they are not the same.

So, in the last part of this chapter, I would like to suggest some ways of thinking about the spiritual dimension, a Higher Power. For the sake of my agnostic friends, I have tried, wherever it wasn't impossibly awkward, to avoid using the word *God*. I also do not endorse any particular theological doctrine or religious practice. The simple idea that we all belong to something beyond ourselves will suffice for the sense of meaning that alcoholics and addicts need for a stable and happy recovery.

THINKING ABOUT A HIGHER POWER

A little philosophy inclineth man's mind to atheism,
but depth in philosophy bringeth men's minds about to
religion.

— FRANCIS BACON (1561–1626)

Like many of my contemporaries, I'm afraid I had a rather insipid religious education. Rites were observed, words mouthed, children dutifully dropped off at Sunday school. Our parents' intentions were certainly good, and I don't blame anyone for the fact that it made very little impression on me. But the fact is that none of it spoke to the question that haunted me: Why am I alive? Is life only a game of survival? Win the competition, collect the rewards, and then die? Or was there something else? And if there wasn't, why wouldn't the question leave me alone?

In the end, I turned from religion to science—to biology and medicine—and my question found new life in a nagging preoccupation with the "mind/body problem." With the benefit of hindsight, I see now that my original question about the meaning of life was behind all my career choices, but for a long time I didn't know it. My professional work wasn't an overt search for purposes beyond my own, and yet the question was there, hidden within the daily work of a medical practice and showing itself from time to time in the form of the mind/brain puzzle. Every now and then, it would stop me, and I would wonder how an organ of blood and tissue inside our heads produced the intangible consciousness that allowed us to ask this very question. For a long time, I didn't understand that the heart of the problem was spiritual, not scientific.

What I did learn, as I searched through psychology and neurology for an answer, was that scientific treatments of the question of consciousness (much less consciousness of self) always seemed to fall short. Articles purporting to address the "mystery of the mind" invariably lapsed into the far easier task of reporting "what we now know" about neurons, synapses, cognitive schema, and the like. The question of consciousness itself got lost and never appeared again. It seemed that Einstein was correct when he said that the state of mind that can take things apart and learn about "mechanisms" is not the state of mind that discovers *why* we are driven to understand those mechanisms in the first place. Disappointment in science of this kind led me to some of the modern philosophers who seemed to have thought long and hard about the question. But try as I might, I just couldn't follow them.

Then one day, during a walk on the beach, an answer came to me in a completely unexpected way. It was a magical day at the ocean: the sun, between seasons, no longer burning the skin; the sea breeze a mere whisper. A young woman appeared on the beach with her dog, a black Labrador retriever. Clearly in his prime—perhaps two years old, bounding with energy, beautiful to watch—this dog was the epitome of his breed. The woman picked up a large piece of driftwood and threw it into the water, well beyond the breakers. Without hesitation, the dog leaped into the water, crashed through the waves, swam to the stick, grabbed it in his mouth, paddled back, struggled again through the waves, and laid the stick at his master's feet. She picked it up and threw it out again. And again the dog retrieved it. And again, and again, and again. Each time, the dog's eagerness to retrieve the stick was the same as it had been the first time. Finally, after thirty minutes of throwing the stick, the woman got tired and stopped. The dog looked as if he could have gone on forever. Even as they walked away, he ran in front of her, dropped the stick at her feet, and wagged his tail—"Again?"

This scene, and the joy that dog radiated, stayed with me for many years. It took some time, but with help I came to understand what had been revealed that day. It was really very simple: The dog was full of joy because he was fulfilling his destiny.

No doubt, wild dogs feel some level of contentment after a successful hunt or in playing with their pups, but this was not that. Retrieving his master's stick wasn't the destiny for which biological evolution had prepared his species. Human beings had reshaped what Nature had only hinted at. This creature's joy was the reflection of a higher level of mind, the result of having been worked upon for thousands of years by a higher level of consciousness. Patiently, persistently, human beings had been selecting, breeding, and training his ancestors. Creating him, really. The result was a creature who was not merely a servant but who had also become a friend and a companion capable of sharing some of his master's conscious experience.

The dog himself, of course, has very little understanding of his master's world—her intentions, hopes, and disappointments— but he can share her joy when he fulfills the purpose for which he was created. The whole idea of a Higher Power is the same. Since the beginning of Time, "God as we understand him" has been working at His creation, evolving creatures capable of higher and higher forms of consciousness, capable of serving Him and sharing part of His conscious experience.

What I learned from that day on the beach was that I had been looking for a solution to the "brain/mind" problem in the wrong place. I had assumed, as my scientific education had led me to believe, that the brain somehow "produced" the mind of itself. But I could never find any explanation that included the actual, living experience of my own consciousness. Nothing could be known about consciousness without consciousness it-self. It seemed the ultimate paradox: The mind could perhaps understand the brain but not vice versa.

On the spiritual side, I had had some simplistic familiarity with the idea of God as creator, but it was without depth. Conventional religious ideas often seemed absurd, and I had not studied the great theistic philosophers. But in light of what I'd seen that day on the beach, a whole new understanding of what it means to be a *created being* came to me. Perhaps, just as the dog's mind had been raised to a higher level by his master's mind, human consciousness also has been raised by a level of mind above it. Perhaps a higher intelligence, power, God—call it what you will—has been trying for a long time to lead us to a destiny beyond what biological evolution has brought us to. Maybe the brain doesn't produce the mind at all. Maybe the brain receives it.

C. S. Lewis has argued that the evidence for a mind beyond our own is in the experience of conscience, the sense that we are responsible to something or someone beyond ourselves. This sense of how we *ought* to act—whether or not we succeed in doing so—is so fundamentally and uniquely human that it is the same in all cultures from all times. Customs vary, but conscience is everywhere and always the same. It tells us not to cheat, to keep our promises, to honor and care for elders, children, and the infirm. In short, it urges us to "do unto others as you would have them do unto you." The fact that none of us adheres to these precepts very well is another matter. The point is that we know that we should. That knowledge is the gift and demand of a higher mind.

So, what has all this to do with recovery from addiction? Just this: Without a sense that our purpose as human beings comes through our relation to something beyond ourselves, recovery from addiction will always be tentative. People may well become abstinent, even for long periods, but, without some kind of spiritual awakening, they will not discover and develop those qualities of character that will enable them to find the meaning behind inescapable suffering. It makes sense that they wouldn't. If the relief offered by drugs and alcohol isn't replaced by something far better and utterly reliable, then when suffering comes along, the abstinent addict will feel trapped and resentful. Awakening to the spiritual, then, means growing in awareness that we belong to something beyond ourselves, something for the sake of which suffering and sacrifice make sense.

There are many ways of coming to a spiritual awakening. I stress the 12-step groups here because they are widely available, free, and adapted specifically for recovery from addiction. Other paths are fine as long as they lead to the same end. Also, participation in 12-step work need not exclude any other spiritual endeavor. Many recovering addicts and alcoholics have found entirely new dimensions of meaning in other spiritual practices as a result of their 12-step work.

In summary, then, a spiritual awakening brings the understanding that we are not alive for ourselves alone. We are not even alive simply for our families, our communities, or even the whole human race. We are alive for the purposes of a Higher Power. To the extent that we can recognize the voice of conscience in how we act with our families, our neighbors, our community, and perhaps even humanity as a whole, then the path to meaning becomes clear. Then this Higher Power isn't some airy-fairy grandfather in space. It may be calling to me in the most mundane aspects of daily life, perhaps even through the driver tailgating me on the freeway, the telemarketer calling at dinnertime, or the colleague who is trying to convince me that the search for truth is really just the play of atoms in my brain.

ARE SCIENCE AND SPIRITUALITY COMPATIBLE?

Thus there are two books from whence I collect my divinity. Besides that written one of God, another of His servant, Nature—that universal and public manuscript which lies expanded unto the eyes of all. Those that never saw Him in the one, have discovered Him in the other.

THOMAS BROWNE (1605–1682)

Two sorts of people believe that science and spirituality are incompatible: extreme religious fundamentalists who reject scientific findings as contradicting the literal interpretation of the Bible and scientists unalterably (if unknowingly) devoted to the philosophy of materialism. The former aren't likely to be reading this book, so there is no need to speak to their point of view. The latter at least claim reasoning as an ideal, and the rest of this book is addressed, if not directly to them, then at least to all of the people their philosophy has influenced.

It is impossible not to appreciate and even stand in awe at

the achievements of science in the modern world. Unfortunately, that same awe prevents many people—even the well-educated among them—from thinking critically when scientists begin to talk philosophy. But the truth is that scientists who claim to have "proved" that God does not exist are not bringing forth more science. They are espousing the *religion* of science: scientism. Jacques Monod, winner of the Nobel Prize for his work in molecular biology, provides a spectacular example of scientism when he writes in *Chance and Necessity*:

> Man must at last wake out of his millenary dream and discover his total solitude, his fundamental isolation. He must realize that, like a gypsy, he lives on the boundary of an alien world; a world that is deaf to his music, and as indifferent to his hopes as it is to his sufferings and his crimes.

Monod isn't presenting scientific facts here. Science is a way of learning about the natural world by hypothesis and experimental trial. His statement is pure philosophy, a twist on the rationalist-humanist tradition, a materialist *belief* about things that cannot be proved or disproved by the scientific method. Dr. Monod and his like-minded colleagues are certainly entitled to their views; only let's be clear that they are beliefs, not scientific facts.

In the end, there are really only two ways of thinking about ourselves and the universe we live in: Either it all "just happened" or it is a creation. The first view is materialistic; the second, spiritual. Either, as Dr. Monod suggests, the origin of the universe, life, human consciousness has been an accident or it has not. Either it has a purpose or it does not. If it has no purpose, then it has no meaning. And here, materialism runs up against a fatal flaw, because asserting anything about the universe is itself a part of that universe. So, if the universe is fundamentally without meaning, then saying so is also meaningless. In other words, it makes no sense to say the universe makes no sense. If, on the other hand, the universe has a purpose, if it is not an accident, then it is the work of a creator whose aims it was intended to fulfill.

Neither view is incompatible with current scientific evidence, which suggests that, beginning with the Big Bang, matter in chaos has been slowly organizing into galaxies, solar systems, organisms, and human beings. Both views are also consistent with the law of entropy: that at the end of time all this order will have wound back down into chaos. If a Higher Power, who is, by definition, *outside* of space and time, chooses to use evolution to create a universe *within* space and time, presumably it can. Perhaps even repeatedly.

So, which is true—materialism or spirituality? Materialism is self-contradictory, but spirituality cannot be proven through any sensory evidence. Nothing we see, hear, touch, or smell—not even as enhanced through the finest scientific instruments—can tell us whether or not something exists beyond them. Material facts, by definition, are limited by space and time and therefore cannot explain anything outside of space and time. At the same time, thinking about those facts, as the quote from Thomas Browne suggests, is useful.

When it keeps to its proper domain—the level of materiality—

the scientific method and the technology it produces cannot be faulted. For those who recognize its limitations and who also retain a sense of wonder and humility, scientific study can bring all the joys associated with music, drama, literature, and the other arts. It represents a vast body of knowledge about how things appear to our senses, and whatever else we may be, we are sensual creatures. Biology, psychology, and medical science do have something to tell us about what we are and where we came from, but it is not what Dr. Monod suggests.

In this spirit, I want to present two ideas based on the science of biology that are helpful in thinking about a Higher Power. There are many more (physicists seem to find them fairly often), but these are two I know enough about to share. But, again, let's be clear. These ideas are no more "provable" by the scientific method than what Dr. Monod is asserting; they are bits of spiritual philosophy based on the proposition that beyond the material universe we can know through the senses, there is another dimension we can know through reason. Finally, at the end of the chapter, I will suggest how this dimension may be known to us directly, in our own consciousness.

"AS ABOVE, SO BELOW"

It is ironic that the "big picture" of life as revealed to us by modern biology should bring us back to something so old. Nevertheless, the ancient phrase "As above, so below" describes very well the pattern of analogous organization at different levels of life, one the late Gregory Bateson would have called a "pattern that connects."

Just as our bodies function by virtue of the work of separate organs and organ systems, so too the cells that exist within those organs have miniature organs of their own. These organelles (the nucleus, mitochondria, ribosomes, and endoplasmic reticulum, etc.) serve the next highest level of being, the cell, in ways entirely analogous to the ways in which our organs serve us. The nucleus of an individual cell, for example, receives and provides the information required for that cell's specialized development and function. At the level of an individual human being, the central nervous system plays the same role, coordinating the perceptions and actions that make each of us a unique human being. Another example: At the cellular level, organelles called mitochondria capture and store energy; at the higher level of the individual organism, the gastrointestinal and hepatic organ systems perform the same function.

These "As above, so below" analogies also extend upward from the level of individuals to the level of life on the planet as a whole. Ecosystems—for example, a prairie or a rain forest— can be regarded as organs of the higher-level creature called "life on Earth." The grasses, shrubs, and trees receive, transform, and store the energy of the sun, performing the same role that mitochondria and the gastrointestinal system play at their levels. This being, "life on Earth," or the "biosphere," as the Russian scientist V. I. Vernadsky called it, certainly seems capable of demonstrating at least one familiar characteristic of organisms: illness. Global warming and the accelerating destruction of rich and diverse ecosystems seem an indisputable example of something gone terribly wrong on a very large scale. As with people, it often takes an illness to make us aware of the harmony of parts that was a healthy organism.

The harmonious coordination of parts that is a living being results from two seemingly paradoxical demands. They are so obvious that we don't often ponder their significance. First, each organ must remain unalterably dedicated to its own role— that is, it must be "true to itself." The liver does not take on the work of the brain, the eyes do not hear, and so on. Yet at the same time, the degree of activity of each organ (its rate or "tempo") must be exquisitely sensitive and obedient to the needs of the whole. Though much remains unknown, biomedical research has puzzled out many of the mechanisms by which the body achieves a stable balance of each of these organs' functions. This balance, or homeostasis, as it was named by the great French physiologist Claude Bernard, is made possible primarily by a collection of glands (the endocrine system) and a complex web of electrically excitable cells (the autonomic nervous system) that respond to the external world through the central nervous system.

Seated at the base of the forebrain, the pituitary gland orchestrates the activity of the other endocrine glands (the thyroid, the adrenals, and the islets of Langerhans in the pancreas, among others). Responding to stimuli from the external world (as interpreted by the brain/mind) and to changes in the internal milieu (through continuous sampling of the bloodstream), it produces "releasing factors," which, in turn, control rates of production of other endocrine hormones in the bloodstream. After being received by special molecules in the membranes of target-organ cells, these hormones, chemical messengers "from above," so to speak, stimulate the release of special chemicals (cyclic nucleotides) within the cell itself. These "second messengers," in turn, then influence intracellular activities that collectively determine rates of growth and metabolism for the organism as a whole.

The autonomic nervous system follows essentially the same pattern except that the interconnecting messages are conducted far more rapidly by means of electrical impulses. This system, divided into two opposing subsystems called the sympathetic and parasympathetic, regulates heart and respiratory rates, blood pressure, sweating, and so forth, by a combination of hormonelike neurotransmitters (notably adrenaline and acetylcholine) and electrical impulses.

As interesting as the details of these systems may be, we are still only describing mechanisms. It is much more important not to lose the big picture, to see the pattern as it is repeated through several levels of life. The pattern is that a lower level of organization is so organized as to be governed by a higher one.

Remarkably, even though Dr. Monod's own scientific work has been instrumental in revealing the details of this pattern, his belief system excludes these analogies and their implication for the meaning of human life. He would, I imagine, dismiss the idea of "As above, so below" as mere fantasy. For him, the appearance of self-consciousness, the appearance of reason and conscience in human beings, means nothing in relation to a higher level of life. In refusing to accept the possibility of a level of mind above our own, however, Dr. Monod and his materialist allies are left with the impossible task of explaining how consciousness (including their own), which is not matter, "arises" from matter.

The simplest materialist solution (put forward by some behaviorists) is to deny that consciousness exists at all, but this is absurd. The advocate of such extreme materialism has to include his own thoughts and feelings among those activities of the brain that are "merely chemistry." He ends up with nonsense, arguing that argument is meaningless.

A more subtle materialist solution to the appearance of consciousness from matter is really a form of avoiding the question altogether. This argument holds that self-consciousness "evolves" gradually from lower forms of consciousness. Besides leaving the human capacity for reason unexplained, this position also reduces the differences of conscious experience between living things—love, hatred, even the sense of self—to mere quantity. Our consciousness is just more of what other primates and mammals—indeed, what all other animals—already have. But does that explain anything? Take the argument down the scale of matter: Are consciousness, reason, and conscience "in" the atoms that became molecules that became organisms that became you and me and Dr. Monod? Was all that already "there" in infinitesimally small particles simply waiting to be added up? It's like saying that the dog on the beach evolved into his special role as a retriever entirely on his own, without any influence from the human beings for whom he was going to do the very retrieving.

In Dr. Monod's philosophy, then, the pattern "As above, so below" does not apply to individual human beings as we actually experience our lives. In the philosophy of materialism, there is no qualitative difference among creatures' consciousness. There is only quantity: more or less of this or that biological material, which somehow adds up to more or less consciousness. Precisely how more and more of the same thing produces something entirely different is regarded as self-evident and fully explained by the principle of gradual accumulation.

When materialists do accept the difficulties of these questions, they often fall back on the call for further research. But more research conducted on the same foundation can never succeed. How can research that is restricted to the investigation of matter ever learn anything about what is not matter? It's a stunning paradox: The man doing the research on how the brain works cannot, by the same methods, learn *why* he is doing it. Nevertheless, nothing is impossible to the human mind enthralled by materialism and the dream of unlimited progress it promises. The whole enterprise can only spin itself, and the rest of us with it, into oblivion. How could it be otherwise? If human beings live in "fundamental isolation," then there is no level of consciousness above our own. We are then responsible only to ourselves, meaning to what is conventional, habitual, or, worse, merely fashionable.

By contrast, spiritually based teachings assert that the universe is organized hierarchically. Consciousness isn't manufactured from a lower level but is received from a higher one. Yes, we are animals made of flesh and blood like all the other animals. In this Dr. Monod is correct. But we are also spiritual beings, creatures endowed with self-consciousness, reason, and conscience. As a result of this higher kind of consciousness, we suffer the knowledge of our mortality. We also search for the meaning of our existence and come to understand that we are meant to serve a Higher Power in some way other animals are not. Here again the analogy "As above, so below" is helpful.

We ourselves have tiny collections of cells (Meissner's corpuscles) in the tips of our fingers, which respond to slight variations of pressure. By sending this information back to the central nervous system, these individual cells serve the level above them, the organism as a whole. Their special sensitivity and capacity for communication is not given to the other cells around them. Those cells have their own special jobs; all support one another. But if the Meissner corpuscles fail to perform their role, the fingers can no longer feel, the hand becomes nearly useless, and an entire universe of human capabilities is lost.

Our capacity for consciousness of self makes us unique among all other creatures on Earth.* If the pattern "As above, so below" is true, then our capacity for this level of consciousness must mean something for the whole organism called "life on Earth." It must also mean something for whatever Higher Power created it all. Precisely what it means is mankind's oldest and most important question.

As I said, for me and for a long time, this question took the form of the brain/mind question: How is consciousness, which itself is not material, related to the material body? Put another way: How can something come from nowhere? The short an-

---

*Recently, scientists have demonstrated that some of the higher animals, notably some primates and elephants, probably experience some rudimentary form of self-consciousness. An elephant, for example, will touch a spot of paint on its forehead when looking at itself in a mirror. But this behavior is a result of contact with human beings; none of these animals in the "natural" state shows any evidence of self-consciousness. In fact, these experiments support the idea that higher states of consciousness are received from a higher level (in this case, human), not "produced" from a lower one.

swer is that it doesn't. Something always comes from somewhere and something else; the original something is perhaps inaccessible to our senses, but it exists. Nothing can yield only nothing.

Common experience raises these questions. Science confirms that they are profoundly perplexing. Mathematics, "the queen of the sciences," can help us toward an answer.

SOMETHING FROM NOTHING:
MIND, BRAIN, AND A HIGHER DIMENSION

One of the simplest ways of thinking about the brain/mind question is by means of the radio/music analogy alluded to earlier in this chapter. Readers who would like to pursue a broader exploration of the ideas behind it may wish to read the highly accessible book by Rupert Sheldrake titled *A New Science of Life*.

The essential idea in this analogy is that the brain doesn't "make" or "produce" consciousness any more than the radio "creates" Beethoven's Ninth. On a literal level, it is, of course, true that the radio is "making" the music, a view perhaps permissible for children or someone utterly ignorant of modern technology. And yet this is just the idea that many modern scientists endorse, perhaps without realizing it, when they declare that mind "arises from" matter. They aren't thinking about where it originates; they are thinking only about where it appears.

It is as though a group of primitive tribesmen stumbled upon a working radio. Being very clever people, they soon learn how to take it apart and put it back together. In time, they become experts in how all the parts fit together, and sometimes, when a part comes loose, they can even fix it. A few of the more imaginative of the tribe dream of making radios for themselves, and some of the more philosophically inclined take up the question of where precisely the music is located inside these radios. Obviously, the music is somewhere inside it; any fool can see that the music isn't coming out of the log the radio is sitting on!

Of course, those of us who have lived with radios since we were children know that radios don't create the music coming out of them. It doesn't produce something out of nowhere; it receives something that originates somewhere else. It then transforms that imperceptible "something" (information encoded in electromagnetic radiations) into a form that can be perceived by the human ear (sound waves). The radio isn't a creator; it is a transformer, a bridge, an instrument that spans two different levels of reality. Perhaps, in the same way, the brain only "produces" consciousness in the literal sense—that is, the brain is where mind appears. Perhaps the brain, like the radio, is also a receiver and transformer.

In 1912, the mathematician-philosopher P. D. Ouspensky wrote about just such questions—the problem of "something from nothing"—and placed spiritual philosophy on a foundation consistent with modern science. In *Tertium Organum*, he explored how phenomena like the otherwise inexplicable appearance of consciousness "from" matter could be approached by positing another dimension beyond the three that we know through the senses. Reasoning by analogy from how beings (living or otherwise) belonging to a higher dimension would appear to beings in a lower dimension, he showed how the appearance of "something from nowhere" is really an illusion based on limited consciousness. In passing through a world of fewer dimensions, an object (living or otherwise) in a higher dimension comes from nowhere and then sometime later disappears back into nothingness. This same movement of a higher dimensional object through a lower dimensional world can also give the illusion of development or evolution.

A circle, for example, is a two-dimensional cross section of a three-dimensional object: a cylinder. A creature living in the lower world of two dimensions, unable to perceive the higher three-dimensional world, would experience the cylinder passing through its world only as a circle coming from nowhere and then, sometime later, disappearing into nothingness. The circle would have "lived and died," so to speak, *on* the dimension below it, while all the time having existed as a whole, and continuing to exist, *in* its own three-dimensional world. If the shape of the cylinder were irregular, then, from the limited perspective of a two-dimensional being, the circle would appear to have changed: to arise, evolve, and, finally, to vanish. The passage of the cylinder through the lower dimension might even in some way change it, or, to draw an analogy, coat it with a color, for example. This is precisely the kind of phenomena that characterize the appearance and evolution of consciousness.

Again, scientists schooled in materialism explain consciousness as the "adding up" of countless complex chemical interactions. Without doubt, these interactions are taking place, and biochemistry does provide one sort of explanation. The electronic circuits in the radio do explain, in a way, "why" we hear Beethoven's Ninth. But this sort of explanation is that of mechanism; the question "why" is really being used to mean "how." In that sense, it is right to say that we hear the music "because" the radio receives certain kinds of electromagnetic radiations, transforms them into electrical impulses, transmits those impulses to a speaker, and so on. But this kind of explanation doesn't tell us anything about what we experience when we hear it, *why* we want to listen to it, and what it *means* to us when we do. Chemical interactions in the brain cannot "add up" to something that isn't chemical.

The material and spiritual levels are not opposites. Both exist, but they are not the same. Material forms that appear to come from "nothing" and disappear to "nowhere" can be thought of as three-dimensional cross sections of four-dimensional objects. As three-dimensional beings, we don't ordinarily perceive this higher dimension. In truth, we can hardly even imagine it. And more and more information isn't going to solve the problem. "Proof" of a higher dimension cannot be found by the methods of science; it requires a higher state of consciousness.

Actually, we already understand this idea in principle. Asleep in bed at night, for example, you may smell the smoke from a fire in your kitchen, but until you wake up from your dream about a forest fire, you cannot save yourself. In the same way, through thought, we can open the rational mind to an acceptance of its own limitations and awaken to the possibility of a higher dimension. Then, as the sages, saints, and mystics have taught from the beginning of time, we will understand that that dimension can only be found within us. It is where we can find direct knowledge of something emerging from nowhere.

EVIDENCE OF A HIGHER DIMENSION: THE PRESENT MOMENT

For the Present is the point at which time touches eternity.

—C. S. LEWIS

As interesting as thinking about a higher dimension may be, ideas do not carry the force of direct experience. A real moment of clarity, the kind of realization that can change a life, does not come from the intellect alone. At the same time, the experience of a higher dimension isn't so far removed from our daily lives. It's manifest right here, right now as I sit writing and you sit reading in the actuality of the present moment.

If we are honest, we have to admit that we rarely live in the present moment but, instead, pass much of our time in the hazy world of passive imagination: daydreaming about the future, ruminating over the past, or simply being swept away in the stream of accidental associations careening around in our minds. Nevertheless, it is also true that many people have had, at least once in their lives, some inkling of a higher reality, of being so intensely alive in the present moment that it was unmistakably different from everything else experienced before it.

The first time it happened to me I was fifteen years old, stuffed into the backseat of a friend's station wagon with the surfboards, a child of privilege on the way to the beach. I claim no credit for it, and I don't recall being particularly happy or unhappy, worried or relaxed. In fact, nothing that preceded that moment gave any indication that it was coming. I simply saw an old man walking along the side of the road, stooped over, leaning on his cane. Suddenly, the moment overwhelmed me with a vast new consciousness. I was flooded with feelings of sadness and tenderness and longing all wrapped up together, and I began to weep to myself. I had no idea what it meant, but I knew it was important and promised that I would never forget that old man. I knew I was being called to something, but I didn't know what.

We aren't able to command such experiences, but consistent efforts (through prayer, meditation, and contemplation) to stop the incessant flow of involuntary associations and to attend to what is in the present moment, here and now, can bring us back to a taste of it. And, slowly, a shocking revelation emerges: The present moment itself doesn't change. What is *in* the present moment—the objects of awareness—change, but the present moment itself does not. Whenever we come back to the present moment, it is still the present moment. There is no other. There never was and there never will be. Time has passed between leaving and returning to it, but being present itself has not changed.

In the analogy of dimensions, we might describe the objects of awareness as the changing cross sections of forms that are themselves whole and unchanging in a higher dimension. Or we could use a Buddhist analogy: that awareness is like the space contained by a bowl. Objects, things, may be placed in or taken out of the bowl, and the size of the bowl may vary, but the quality or character of space contained by the bowl does not change. That which does not change we call eternal.

The state of consciousness to which Nature and evolution has brought us, and which differs from that of animals only in amount and not in kind, is more or less automatic, determined, and conditioned by external stimuli. In this, the behaviorists and biochemists are right in their characterization of human beings as complex biopsychosocial machines. Heredity gives us a whole repertoire of potentials: to speak, to stand, to play, to mate, and all the rest. As a result of these instinctive drives and appetites, our attention is drawn to the various objects that satisfy them, and a certain pleasure or happiness is our reward. In this sense, the child's instinctive joy at standing up or solving a puzzle differs only in degree, not in quality, from his parents' joy at seeing the same child graduate from college. Wonderful feelings, to be sure—I've had them myself—but they are temporal, not eternal. And, apparently by some kind of cosmic law, the sum of temporal happiness seems just about balanced by an equal degree of unhappiness, the inevitable feelings of frustration, sadness, and disappointment that come with failure, misfortune, and illness.

Against all this stands the strangely unchanging, timeless present moment. Though we may come to it unexpectedly in moments of mortal danger, intense excitement, or even intoxication, life itself does not require us to remember it and wonder at it. Without thinking about what it means, human beings remain the paragon of animals, the most successful (at least as we ourselves define *success*) species on Earth, the ultimate predator, capable of changing the environment to ensure survival in ways no other animal ever has. But if we do remember it and work at understanding it, then the experience of the present moment awakens a strange longing, an unexpected homesickness, for the eternal.

You would think that having once had a powerful experience of this kind, no one would ever forget it, that we would long to remember it, to find it again, but it is not so. We do forget. Perhaps no one ever taught us what it meant or even confirmed that it was significant. Without guidance, without work toward remembering this experience of a higher dimension, we remain attached (Buddhist) or identified (Gurdjieff) with the objects of awareness and live passively in a lower, automatized state of consciousness, without even a memory of the transcendent joy that could make suffering meaningful.

Experiences of a higher consciousness simply do not last. Remembering the eternal dimension by attending to the present moment requires effort. Learning to live in it demands unending effort. That is why there is no external manipulation—no electronic device, no pharmaceutical wonder drug, no brilliant new psychotherapeutic technique—more helpful to recovering alcoholics and addicts than sharing their "strength, hope, and experience" with one another. Their example can remind the rest of us that we are all immersed in a great mystery, that we all belong to something greater than ourselves, and that forgetfulness is the chief cause of our unnecessary suffering. Please note the word *unnecessary*. Some suffering we cannot and must not try to avoid, but surely we are not required to add more misery of our own making.

I hope I've made the larger point of this last chapter clear. The problem of addiction is not someone else's problem: some poor victim of bad genes, a crazy family, or lousy socioeconomic status. It is my problem—not in some metaphorical sense but literally, actually. From the point of view of the spiritual, eternal dimension, we are all addicted: to career, to possessions, to self-image, to comfort, and especially to suffering of our own making. The unthinking effort so characteristic of so many modern enterprises, both personal and collective, to eliminate any and all suffering, in the end, only makes things worse.

If we would listen to the saints, the philosophers, the mystics, and the poets, we would hear that the obstacle to understanding our suffering lies within us, that the truth has been in front of us all along. We cannot eliminate all suffering. It's not that we need to know more. We don't need a better pill or a more ingenious procedure. We need to awaken to the eternal presence that gives our suffering meaning.

How each person should approach this work of awakening is not a matter I would advise in a book. But, in general, for people with a readily identifiable addiction, the 12-step groups are an excellent place to begin. For the rest of us, I know a few things. I know it cannot be done alone. Alone, I can develop such fantasies as to make a sage weep. Alone, I can become capable of an imaginary "unconditional love" that evaporates the moment someone cuts me off on the freeway. Alone, I don't owe anybody anything.

But I also know that with good guidance and persistent efforts, I can acknowledge my powerlessness and surrender my willfulness. In small steps, always and only here and now, I can make myself available to be worked upon by an intelligence beyond my own. I know that growing in conscious awareness of this Higher Power means that my small steps can never be automatic or passive and that no one else can take them for me. I know I'll often fail to hit the mark, but I know too that the choice will be offered again and again, and again, and again. Apparently, this master never tires of throwing the stick.

Years ago, one of my principal teachers told a group of us about a certain custom among Central Asian travelers who happen to meet at the top of a mountain pass. As usual, I didn't understand it very well at the time, but now, in view of this endlessly patient Higher Power, in view of the never-ending possibility of choosing to retrieve the stick, I begin to understand the point. It seems that when they meet, these travelers say to one another, "Brother, may you never tire."

References

As I indicated in my preface, I did not cite my sources in individual footnotes throughout the body of the text. Instead, I list here at the end what seemed the most important and relevant books on my shelves. Many contain articles by several different authors. In any case, this list is neither comprehensive nor up to date. My intention is to credit, as best I can, those whose ideas I have used, not to provide an exhaustive bibliography for academic use.

My sincere apologies to those authors whom I have neglected to include as well as to those who may feel that I have misrepresented their work.

CHAPTER 1. IS ADDICTION A DISEASE?

Alcoholics Anonymous, 4th ed. (New York: Alcoholics Anonymous World Services, 2001).

American Psychiatric Association. *Diagnostic and Statistical Manual*, 3rd ed. (Washington, DC: APA, 1980).

Bargh, J. A., and T. L. Chartrand, "The Unbearable Automaticity of Being." *American Psychologist* 54 (1999): 462–79.

Berger, C. S. *Substance Abuse as Symptom* (Hillsdale, NJ: The Analytic Press, 1991).

Davies, D. L. "Normal Drinking in Recovered Alcohol Addicts," *Quarterly Journal of Studies on Alcohol* 23 (1962): 94–104.

Edwards, G., and M. Lader. *The Nature of Drug Dependence* (New York: Oxford University Press, 1990).

Fingarette, H. *Heavy Drinking: The Myth of Alcoholism as a Disease* (Berkeley: The University of California Press, 1988).

Gallant, D. M. *Alcoholism: A Guide to Diagnosis, Intervention and Treatment* (New York: W. W. Norton, 1987).

Goodwin, D. W. *Is Alcoholism Hereditary?* (New York: Oxford University Press, 1976).

Guidano, V. F., and G. Liotti. *Cognitive Processes and Emotional Disorders* (New York: The Guilford Press, 1983).

Jellinek, E. M. *The Disease Concept of Alcoholism* (New Haven: Yale College and University Press, 1960).

Johnson, V. *I'll Quit Tomorrow* (San Francisco: Harper & Row, 1980).

Ludwig, Arnold M. *Understanding the Alcoholic's Mind: The Nature of Craving and How to Control It* (New York: Oxford University Press, 1988).

Orford, J., and G. Edwards. *Alcoholism* (New York: Oxford University Press, 1977).

Pattinson, E. M., M. B. Sobell, and L. C. Sobell. *Emerging Concepts of Alcohol Dependence* (New York: Springer, 1977).

Peele, Stanton. *The Meaning of Addiction: Compulsive Experience and Its Interpretation* (Lexington, MA: Lexington Books, 1986).

Shuckit, M. A. *Drug and Alcohol Abuse* (New York: Plenum Press, 1984).

Stillings, N. A., et al. *Cognitive Science: An Introduction* (Cambridge, MA: The MIT Press, 1987).

Twelve Steps and Twelve Traditions (New York: Alcoholics Anonymous World Services, 1952).

Uleman, J. S., and J. A. Bargh, eds. *Unintended Thought* (New York: The Guilford Press, 1989).

Vaillant, G. *The Natural History of Alcoholism* (Cambridge, MA: Harvard University Press, 1983).

CHAPTER 2. WHY ME?

American Psychiatric Association. *Diagnostic and Statistical Manual of Mental Disorders,* 4th ed. (Washington, DC: APA, 1994).

Ashton, H., and R. Stepney. *Smoking: Psychology and Pharmacology* (London: Tavistock, 1982).

Barrows, S., and R. Rosen, eds. *Drinking: Behavior and Belief in Modern History* (Berkeley: University of California Press, 1983).

Bean, M. H., and N. Zinberg. *Dynamic Approaches to the Understanding and Treatment of Alcoholism* (New York: Free Press, 1981).

Blane, H. T., and K. E. Leonard. *Psychological Theories of Drinking and Alcoholism* (New York: The Guilford Press, 1987).

Callahan, D. *Problem Drinkers: A National Survey* (San Francisco: Jossey Bass, 1970).

Estes, N. J., and M. E. Heinemann, eds. *Alcoholism: Development, Consequences, and Interventions* (St. Louis: C. V. Mosby, 1986).

Goldstein, A. *Molecular and Cellular Aspects of the Drug Addictions* (New York: Springer-Verlag, 1989).

Hollingshead, A. B., and F. C. Redlich. *Social Class and Mental Illness* (New York: John Wiley & Sons, 1958).

Kammeier, M. L., H. Hoffman, and R. G. Loper. "Personality Characteristics of Alcoholics as College Freshmen and at Time of Treatment," *Quarterly Journal of Studies on Alcohol* 34 (1973): 390–399.

McKim, W. A. *Drugs and Behavior: An Introduction to Behavioral Pharmacology* (Englewood Cliffs, NJ: Prentice-Hall, 1986).

Meyer, R. E. *Psychopathology and Addictive Behaviors* (New York: The Guilford Press, 1986).

Pavlov, I. P. *Conditioned Reflexes* (New York: Dover Publications, 1927).

Pittman, D. J., and C. R. Snyder. *Society, Culture and Drinking Patterns* (New York: John Wiley & Sons, 1962).

Weil, A., and W. Rosen. *Chocolate to Morphine* (Boston: Houghton Mifflin, 1983).

CHAPTER 3. DOES TREATMENT "WORK"?

Armor, D. J., J. M. Polich, and H. B. Stanbul. *Alcoholism and Treatment* (New York: John Wiley & Sons, 1978).

Brown, S. *Treating the Alcoholic* (New York: John Wiley & Sons, 1980).

Frank, J. D. *Persuasion and Healing: A Comparative Study of Psychotherapy* (Baltimore: Johns Hopkins University Press, 1981).

Giltlow, S., and S. Peyser. *Alcoholism: A Practical Treatment Guide* (Philadelphia: Grune & Stratton, 1988).

Kinney, J. *Loosening the Grip* (New York: McGraw-Hill, 2000).

Lowinson, J. H., P. Ruiz, R. B. Millman, and J. G. Langrod. *Comprehensive Textbook on Substance Abuse* (Baltimore: Williams & Wilkins, 1992).

Marlatt, G. A., and J. R. Gordon, eds. *Relapse Prevention* (New York: The Guilford Press, 1985).

Miller, W. R., and N. Heather. *Treating Addictive Behavior* (New York: Plenum Press, 1986).

O'Brien, Charles. "The Mosaic of Addiction," *American Journal of Psychiatry* 161, no. 10 (2004): 1742.

Pendery, M. L., I. M. Maltzman, and L. J. West. "Controlled Drinking by Alcoholics? New Findings and a Reevaluation of a Major Affirmative Study," *Science* 217 (1982): 169–175.

Sobell, M. B., and L. C. Sobell. "Alcoholics Treated by Individualized Behavior Therapy: One Year Treatment Outcome," *Behavior Research and Therapy* 11 (1973): 599–618.

CHAPTER 4. IS A SPIRITUAL AWAKENING NECESSARY FOR RECOVERY?

Bateson, G. *Mind and Nature: A Necessary Unity* (Cresskill, NJ: Hampton Press, 1979).

_____. *Steps to an Ecology of Mind* (New York: Ballantine Books, 1972).

Cannon, W. B. *The Wisdom of the Body* (New York: W. W. Norton, 1932).

Daumal, R. *Mount Analogue* (Boston: Shambala, 1992).

Deikman, A. *The Observing Self* (Boston: Beacon Press, 1982).

Ehrenfeld, David. *The Arrogance of Humanism* (New York: Oxford University Press, 1978).

Gurdjieff, G. I. *Beelzebub's Tales to His Grandson: All and Everything* (New York: E. P. Dutton, 1950).

_____. *Meetings with Remarkable Men* (New York: E. P. Dutton, 1952).

James, W. *The Varieties of Religious Experience* (New York: Penguin, 1982).

King, C. Daly. *The States of Human Consciousness* (New Hyde Park, NY: University Press, 1963).

Lewis, C. S. *Mere Christianity* (San Francisco. HarperCollins Edition, 2001).

_____. *The Problem of Pain* (San Francisco: HarperCollins Edition, 2001).

_____. *The Screwtape Letters* (San Francisco: HarperCollins Edition, 2001).

Lindesmith, Alfred. *The Addict and the Law* (Bloomington: Indiana University Press, 1965).

Monod, J. *Chance and Necessity: An Essay on the Natural Philosophy of Modern Biology* (New York: Alfred A. Knopf, 1971).

Needleman, Jacob. *Sin and Scientism* (San Francisco: Robert Briggs Associates, 1985).

_____. *The Way of the Physician* (New York: Harper & Row, 1985).

Ouspensky, P. D. *In Search of the Miraculous* (New York: Harcourt, Brace, 1949).

_____. *Tertium Organum*, 3rd American ed. (New York: Alfred A. Knopf, 1969).

Sheldrake, R. *A New Science of Life* (London: Blond and Briggs, 1981).

Starr, P. *The Social Transformation of American Medicine* (New York: Basic Books, 1982).

Tart, Charles, ed. *Altered States of Consciousness: A Book of Readings* (New York: John Wiley & Sons, 1969).

Twersky, A. *Addictive Thinking*, 2nd ed. (Center City, MN: Hazelden PES, 1997).

Vayesse, J. *Toward Awakening* (New York: Harper & Row, 1979).

Vernadsky, V. I. *The Biosphere* (New York: Springer-Verlag, 1997).

Wilbur, K., J. Engler, and D. P. Brown. *Transformations of Consciousness* (Boston and London: Shambala, 1986).

Index

recovery (*cont.*)
    participation in 12-step program, 94
    responsibility for, 6, 69, 114
    restoration of choice, 73
    seed analogy, 129–31
    spiritual awakening as key to, 114, 156
    spiritual dimension of, 137–39
    stages of, 130–31
    willingness to make difficult choices, 116, 123
    See also treatment
Redgate, Tom, x, 98, 145–46
relapse
    abstinence without spiritual awakening, 142–44
    addiction as relapsing brain disease, 31–32, 93
    as choice, 93–94
    discontinuation of 12-step participation, 88–89
    forgetting or not caring, 89–93
    inevitability of, 32–33, 93
    reawakening of automatism, 24–25
    as spiritual problem, 122
research on addiction
    addictive personality, 63–64
    adoptee studies, 47–48
    approach to addiction as single process, 75–76
    "blind men and the elephant" analogy, 41–43
    confusion of behavior with disease, 76–77
    diagnosis by adverse consequences, 77–79
    disciplinary specialization, 42
    retrospective approach, 43
    statistical manipulation, 85
    twins, studies on, 49–50
    unclear diagnosis criteria, 75
    See also Vaillant, George
resistance
    germ theory, 38–40
    tolerance to addictive drugs, 21–23, 51, 102
    See also susceptibility

responsibility
    avoidance of, 61, 93, 146
    for dealing with addiction, 6, 69, 114
    to Higher Power, 155, 165
    See also choice
Revia (naltrexone), 122, 124
risk of addiction. *See* susceptibility

Schick method of aversive conditioning, 81
science
    "as above, so below" conceptualization, 160–63
    compatibility with spirituality, 157–60
    materialist approach to concept of consciousness, 163–65, 169–70
    See also medical profession; research on addiction
Seconal withdrawal, 102–4
sedatives, withdrawal from, 102–4
self-centeredness and narcissism, 60–61, 112
Silkworth, William, 12
sobriety. *See* abstinence
social factors
    acceptability of behaviors, 67
    availability of addictive substance, 54, 126–27
    cultural expectations, 55–58
    legality of addictive substance, 31, 61–62, 107, 124
    socioeconomic status, 55, 77–78
sociopathic personality, 65
spiritual awakening
    compatibility of spirituality and science, 157–60
    as key to recovery, 114, 156
    meaning, definition of, 135–36
    moment of clarity, 145–46, 171
    as path to meaning of suffering, 142, 156–57
    present moment, experience and recollection of, 171–74
    recovery, definition of, 137–39
    search for, through 12-step programs, 142

About the Author

Richard S. Sandor, M.D., is a board-certified psychiatrist with more than twenty-five years' experience in the addiction field. He has served as the medical director of several different drug and alcohol treatment programs in Southern California, including Redgate Memorial Recovery Center, the Sepulveda VA Medical Center, the Betty Ford Center (L.A. outpatient program), and Saint John's Hospital in Santa Monica. He was on the clinical faculty of UCLA and was president of the California Society of Addiction Medicine from 1993 to 1995. A graduate of Yale and the USC School of Medicine, Dr. Sandor received his psychiatric training at the UCLA Neuropsychiatric Institute and is now in private practice in Santa Monica.